STUDIES IN HISTORY, ECONOMICS, AND PUBLIC LAW

EDITED BY THE FACULTY OF POLITICAL SCIENCE
OF COLUMBIA UNIVERSITY

Number 311

OUTDOOR RECREATION LEGISLATION AND
ITS EFFECTIVENESS

OUTDOOR RECREATION LEGISLATION AND ITS EFFECTIVENESS

A Summary of American Legislation for Public
Outdoor Recreation, 1915–1927, together with a Study
of the Association between Recreation Areas and
Juvenile Delinquency in Manhattan, 1920

BY

ANDREW G. TRUXAL

AMS PRESS
NEW YORK

98142

COLUMBIA UNIVERSITY
STUDIES IN THE
SOCIAL SCIENCES

311

The Series was formerly known as
Studies in History, Economics and Public Law

Reprinted with the permission of Columbia University Press
From the edition of 1929, New York
First AMS EDITION published 1968
Manufactured in the United States of America

Library of Congress Catalogue Card Number: 68-58630

AMS PRESS, INC.
NEW YORK, N.Y. 10003

To
MY WIFE

PREFACE

No apologia is necessary for undertaking a study in the field of public recreation. It has taken its place, and rightly so, among those subjects which are of concern to the sociologist. The phenomenal growth of so-called commercial recreation, notably, the moving pictures and professional sports, has centered popular attention on the problem of providing leisure-time activities for all of the people. The industrialization of our civilization with its concomitant, the shortening of the working day, has led to two important sociological situations. In the first place, it has made possible the concentration of the people in urban centers; in the second place, it has created the problem of having provided the masses with increased leisure for which they were uneducated and unprepared. It was but natural and inevitable that this new situation would be seized upon by commercial interests, and the moving-picture industry together with the promoters of large-scale professional athletic contests have " cashed in " on the new conditions. Only in recent years has there been an effort made to provide in or near urban centers public recreation spaces for the use of the people. And the movement had not gone far before it became apparent that what was needed as much as providing the actual spaces was a slow process of educating the people to prefer participation in recreational activities to watching from the bleachers others perform.

This may well account for the fact that the movement to provide outdoor recreational facilities for children has attained greater proportions than the public provision for adult recreation. Children can be induced, with the proper environmental stimuli, to play. Adults, to whom leisure time is a new acquirement, must be educated to play. The community-center movement, the community forum, the provisions made by industries for recreational activities for their employees, are ways in which the adult problem is being met. But the chief emphasis of the recreational movement has been centered on the children. It is they who will feel in the next generation the full impact of urbanization, industrialization, and leisure time.

The study here undertaken divides itself sharply into two parts. The first part constitutes a summary of the American legislation of the past twelve years (1915 to 1927) making provision for public outdoor recreation. The reasons for the selection of this period were two-fold. In the first place, the interest on the part of the government in the field of public recreation is a comparatively recent phenomenon. With two exceptions, no states in 1915 had enacted legislation empowering municipalities to create recreation departments as integral elements of the city government. In 1927, twenty-one states had such laws. In 1915, while certain cities—Boston, Buffalo, Charleston, Los Angeles, New York City, Oakland, Calif., and Providence, R. I. — had created such departments, the movement had, by no means, become general. As recently as 1921, only twenty-one states had by law created or received as gifts state parks or reservations for recreation. In 1927, thirty-four states had created such areas. The more important reason, however, for the selection of this period, was the fact that in 1915 the Russell Sage Foundation published a pamphlet entitled " Recreation Legislation ", which was a revision to date of a former study made along the same lines. This pamphlet was edited by the Director of Recreation, Lee F. Hanmer, with the collaboration of August H. Brunner, and presented typical features of the legislation then extant.

The second half of this study is in the nature of a scientific exploration. Much has been written but little has been done to discover whether or not the provision of recreational facilities is worth the effort, in terms of the general welfare. A small segment of one problem was chosen for analysis. The question raised was whether or not the occurrence of recreational areas is associated with the incidence of juvenile delinquency. The field of investigation was Manhattan Island. The territory was divided into a number of play districts, in each of which the amount of play space in use in 1920 was related to the number of arrests for delinquency in the same year. A mathematical statement of the amount of this association for the island as a whole was arrived at, and further evidence was gathered concerning certain environmental factors which are supposed to contribute to child delinquency: racial composition of the population, child density per acre and police regulation. The material collected on these latter factors served to check up the conclusions reached by the former comparisons, which revealed a certain amount of association between the presence of supervised play areas and the absence of juvenile delinquency.

Invaluable assistance was given to the author in the preparation of this work by the Department of Recreation of the Russell Sage Foundation. To Mr. Clarence Arthur Perry and Mr. Charles J. Storey, the author is indebted for constructive suggestions; to Miss Marguerita P. Williams for aid in editing the manuscript; and to Mr. Lee F. Hanmer, Director of the Department, for critical reading of the copy and access to all the resources of the Foundation. Thanks are also given to Mr. H. S. Braucher and Mr. Arthur Williams of the Playground and Recreation Association of America, to Mr. H. S. Buttenheim and Mrs. Martha Candler of the American City Bureau, and to Miss Esther Crandell of the National Municipal League, for access to the files of those organizations. Appreciation is also expressed of the help of Mr. Raymond H. Torrey of the American Scenic and Historic Preservation Society for putting the author in touch with state officials interested in the problems of state areas for recreation. Especial gratitude is acknowledged to Professors Lindsay, Tenney, Chaddock and Ross of the Department of Sociology of Columbia University for aid in the molding of the form and content of this dissertation. In a larger way, the writer is indebted to these last-named and to Professor F. H. Giddings for the privileges accompanying their instruction in Sociology during the past three years.

A. G. T.

Columbia University, June, 1928.

CONTENTS

CHAPTER II

The Municipality as the Unit in Conducting a Program of Recreation

CHAPTER V

State and Federal Provisions for Public Outdoor Recreation

PART II

The Social Significance of Recreation

METHODOLOGY EMPLOYED IN PART TWO

CHAPTER VI

Attempts to Evaluate Recreation in Relation to Juvenile Delinquency

CHAPTER VII

ASSOCIATION BETWEEN PLAY AREAS AND DELINQUENCY IN MANHATTAN

PART ONE
AMERICAN LEGISLATION FOR PUBLIC OUTDOOR RECREATION

1915—1927

INTRODUCTION

THE "laissez-faire" attitude in government is gone. Under the stimulus of the Physiocrats, Adam Smith and the English economists of the late eighteenth and early nineteenth centuries, it had its day. But the situation is quite the reverse today. Far from the government adopting a policy of " hands off ", there has been in the past sixty years a decided movement toward governmental regulation of many social and economic activities. Workmen's compensation laws, old-age pensions, factory legislation, legislation in behalf of women and children in industry, these are only a few aspects of this latest venture of the government, initiated on the Continent and only reaching its full force in the United States in the first quarter of the present century.

How is this tendency on the part of the state to take over functions that were formerly private, to be explained? W. Jethro Brown[1] assigns three possible reasons for it: first, " the separation of church and state has been accompanied by a progressive tendency on the part of the state to undertake duties that were formerly a function of the church "; second, " the pressure of social and economic problems "; third, " the progress of a movement (the democratic of the last century) which is one of the most remarkable in history ".

However the movement is to be accounted for, it is an object of no little concern to the sociologist. Professor Franklin H. Giddings thinks it is tending toward a state of

[1] Brown, W. Jethro, *The Underlying Principles of Modern Legislation,* E. P. Dutton & Co., New York, 1915, 315 pp., pp. 283, 284, 314.

" legal villeinage " just as serious in many respects as the economic villeinage of the Middle Age. In this connection he says: [1]

> Governments attempt to standardize not only rights at law but also legal procedure, administrative rules, and the conduct of citizens . . . Trial by jury, however, which mediates between folkways and stateways, is a venerable if not always a venerated defense against the governmentalists, who would dictate and ration our food and drink, write our medical prescriptions, cut our clothes, tell us what we may read and look at, and send us to bed at curfew.

The government, of course, justifies its entrance into these various fields on the basis of the " police power ". It is difficult to define the meaning of that term when applied to the powers of government. Commons and Andrews [2] speak of it as " an indefinite authorization for the American state to abridge liberty or property without consent or compensation in addition to its other more definite powers." It is generally spoken of in the legal profession as the " twilight zone " of legislative power and yet that is probably a misnomer. It is more, as Newman F. Baker [3] says, than a mere residuum of power—it is a power in itself.

The usual definition is that the police power is the power inherent in the government to enact laws, within constitutional limits, to promote the order, safety, health, morals, and general welfare of society . . . The term (police power) was always unfortunate as a readily misleading attempt to give a descriptive label to what is really the unclassified residuum of legislative

[1] Giddings, F. H., *Studies in the Theory of Human Society*, The Macmillan Co., New York, 1922, 308 pp., p. 193.

[2] Commons, John R. and Andrews, John B., *Principles of Labor Legislation*, Harper and Bros., New York, rev. ed., 1927, 616 pp., p. 13.

[3] Baker, Newman F., *Legal Aspects of Zoning*, Univ. of Chicago Press, Chicago, 1927, 182 pp., pp. 15, 26.

power. It is better to conceive of it as an inherent power in the community to satisfy a public need in a reasonable way . . . "The assumption that the police power extends only to the health, safety and morals of the public, which was at one time quite general, is now out of date. The modern view is that the state may control the conduct of individuals by any regulation which upon reasonable grounds can be regarded as adapted to promoting the common welfare, convenience, and prosperity."

This latter statement, quoted from an opinion of the Kansas Court,[1] represents the interpretation which modern jurisprudence is placing upon this power. It also coincides with the statement of Commons and Andrews quoted with regard to this as an "indefinite authorization to abridge liberty and property."

Now one of the fields into which the government has ventured is that of public recreation. When this term is used in this study it is understood to mean those facilities and forms of recreation which are provided wholly or partly at public expense by governmental agencies for the play, amusement or entertainment of the public at large. The dividing line between public recreation and other types of recreation is that which is conventionally understood when public recreation is spoken of as over against professional and commercial recreation. The attitude of the government toward the former is one of promotion; toward the latter, one of regulation.

Public recreation may be divided into two parts: indoor and outdoor. Under the former come recreation and community centers, coliseums and auditoriums, and the community use of school buildings and grounds for public meetings, forums and entertainments. The last of these has been extensively studied by Clarence Arthur Perry,[2] and more

---

[1] 101 Kan. 789, 794. See Noble State Bank *v.* Haskell, 219 U. S. 104.

[2] Perry, Clarence Arthur, *Wider Use of the School Plant*, New York, Survey Associates, 1910, 423 pp.

recently by Eleanor T. Glueck.[1]   These indoor types are excluded from this study, whose emphasis is placed upon public outdoor recreation in such forms as municipal parks and playgrounds, athletic fields, swimming pools, public baths, bathing beaches, bands and concerts, golf courses, tourist camps, and also federal, state and local parks, forests and reservations when used for recreational purposes.   The material, then, that is to form the basis for the subsequent analysis will consist of federal, state and local laws making provisions for public outdoor recreation.

By far the most significant change that has taken place in the past twelve years with respect to legislation for public outdoor recreation has occurred in the attitude of the local community toward the problem.   Prior to 1915, it may fairly be said that most of the recreation legislation was in the nature of state laws granting to local units powers to extend the use of school buildings and grounds to the citizens of the community for recreational purposes.   A few of the cities— Boston, Buffalo, Charleston, Detroit, Los Angeles, New York, Oakland and Providence—had, in response to a felt need, established a government agency as an integral element of the local government with powers to provide a recreational system.   While such cities were not numerous, they represented the beginning of a movement which has become pronounced in recent years and which Joseph Rich Fulk has happily called " the municipalization of play and recreation ".[2]   This movement to place municipal recreation alongside of the local water, fire, and other departments of the city government has progressed in spite of, rather than because of, community sentiment.   It is true that in many

[1] Glueck, Eleanor T., *The Community Use of Schools*, Williams & Wilkins Co., Baltimore, 1927, 222 pp.

[2] Fulk, Joseph Richard, *The Municipalization of Play and Recreation*, University Place, Neb., The Claflin Printing Co., 1922, 97 pp.

communities the need has been experienced and sentiment has been aroused for the creation of such a governmental agency. But others have accepted the movement and have established such departments in order to keep their cities in line with developments elsewhere, only to find that because of the lack of a strong community sentiment this department, being the newest, was the first to suffer in budget-making. In still other municipalities, the situation has been forced on the community by promotive agencies or local groups without adequate emphasis on educating public opinion to the value of such a move. In such places the movement has had indifferent success, depending on local sentiment and local officials.

While it is true that the most progress in legislation for public outdoor recreation has come through the municipal governing body, it is also true that such legislation can only be passed when the states have delegated the powers to the local units. Therefore, it is to be noted that during the past twelve years there has been a large amount of state legislation enacted, the purpose of which has been to grant to municipalities all the powers necessary to establish such recreational agencies. Nor is this the only sphere of activity in which the state legislature has been engaged. While no state has as yet adopted a comprehensive state-wide recreational program, there have been movements along that line. And the state has been active in creating state agencies to accept, administer, develop and coordinate state parks and reservations for recreational purposes. Up to this time the state has not been spending large amounts of public funds for the development of public recreational areas but has, in many cases, relied on gifts of land to augment its park system. However, there is a growing tendency on the part of the state governments to regard the spending of public moneys for recreation purposes as a legitimate and necessary use for such funds. With respect to the federal government, less has been done in the way of legislation for recreation. This branch of government has, up to this time, regarded the provision of local recreation opportunities as primarily a state and local problem.

It would hardly be possible, even if it were useful, to present all the laws that have been passed in even a twelve-year period. The method to be followed, then, in this analysis will be to present typical legislation on each subject considered and follow that with a summary digest of all of the legislation. Several typical measures will be taken up under each head in order to illustrate the varying features of the legislation, from meager to rather complete provisions. In the matter of the local ordinances, there will be one variation in method. To gather together all of the city and town ordinances having to do with recreation would be an impossible task, so the author has selected sixty ordinances which represent cities of different size and which present the important variations in acquisition, administration, and control of recreational areas and has made a summary digest of them. The same procedure has been followed with regard to the mass of state legislation on the subject of state parks and reservations, except that in this case no attempt was made to present in full any state laws.

The student of urban sociology might well wish that our cities had been planned in advance to meet some of the pressing needs of the present congested populations. But in the matter of providing adequate recreational areas in large urban centers, it is too late to hope that the cities can be remade to meet this one need. However, since there is every reason to believe that urbanization will continue, it may be the policy of wisdom partially to " forget those things which are behind " and to plan intelligently for the cities of the future. Such city planning is proceeding apace and every intelligent city planner is taking into consideration the provision for future recreational areas. Legislation with respect to making such provision has been attempted, and with what results will be presented in the first chapter, together with a statement of the whole status of the problem as it relates to planning for recreation spaces in the future American city.

This chapter will be followed by two chapters on the municipality as the unit in the conduct of a system of recreation. Here, the general relations between the local and state governments will be considered, followed by an analysis of state and local legislation covering such subjects as the local department of recreation and its functions, municipal music, municipal tourist camps, and town forests. The discussion of the municipality as the unit will be closed with a chapter on the liabilities of the local government when conducting a recreational program. One additional chapter will be devoted to the federal and state legislative provisions for recreation.

The purpose of making such an analysis of existing legislation is not only theoretical—it is also practical. It should be of value to the public official who is interested in putting his state and locality in line with the developments elsewhere. But while this practical aspect is important, the theoretical problem involved is more important for the sociologist. The student of any social problem has to ask himself two questions: " How did we get that way?" and, " What are we going to do about it?" The analysis of the legislation should answer the first of these two questions. But after the facts are ascertained with regard to this question, the second query must be answered. What justification is there for the enactment of all this legislation covering the field of public recreation? Can it be demonstrated that this expenditure of time and energy is on the whole worth while and for the general welfare? The answer to such a question will be uppermost in the mind of the author in Part Two of this study. An analysis will be made of the association between recreation areas and juvenile delinquency in Manhattan in 1920. The purpose of such an investigation will be to refine the methods by which this and similar problems will have to be attacked in order either to justify or to show unjustifiable the present governmental interest in recreation.

CHAPTER I

RECREATION AS AFFECTED BY CITY PLANNING AND ZONING

LARGE cities, such as New York, Chicago, Boston and Philadelphia, and other smaller urban centers have discovered, much to their regret, that in their most congested areas there are the least public provisions for recreation. Then, as with the proverbial unlocked stable, the administrators seek to undo the mistake by condemning properties worth millions of dollars for the sake of providing a small playground for the children. The William H. Seward Park in lower Manhattan comprises about two acres. If the land had been purchased years ago for the purposes of a future playground, it would have cost the city several hundred dollars. It cost the taxpayers approximately two million dollars. " Chicago and New York each has expended more than $100,000 in the repurchase of waterfront." [1] In the budget for the present year (1928) in New York City, the Board of Estimate has set aside $500,000 for the purpose of buying land for recreational areas in the most congested sections of Manhattan.

Such illustrations could be multiplied. These are sufficient to demonstrate the fact that if the American cities had been planned intelligently fifty years ago, this condition would not be so embarrassing. To obviate such difficulties is the purpose of city planning. It is the control in advance of the growth of the city and an intelligent effort to make provisions within the urban centers for the probable future needs of the population. John Nolen[2] defines it as " the intelli-

[1] *The Playground* for September, 1927, p. 306.

[2] Nolen, John, *New Ideals in the Planning of Cities, Towns and Villages,* American City Bureau, New York, 1919, 139 pp., p. 25.

gent control and guidance of the physical conformation, growth and alteration of cities, towns, or parts thereof, considered in their entirety." While the problem of the provision of recreational facilities is the problem uppermost in this discussion, city planning takes into consideration all of the city's future needs, such as those of traffic, locations of public buildings and other public needs. " A City Plan is concerned chiefly with streets, parks, playgrounds, public buildings and other public spaces both within the present city and throughout the surrounding country over which the city is likely to spread—the metropolitan area." [1]

What, then, has zoning to do with city planning? Whereas the city plan is a guide to the physical conformation of the city, zoning supplements the city plan by regulating the uses to which private land may be put. It has to do not only with the uses of the land but also such subjects as the percentage of lot space that may be occupied by buildings, the height of buildings, and the division of the city into various classes of districts: commercial, industrial, residential and unclassified. " Zoning is the application of common sense and fairness to the public regulations governing the use of private real estate." [2] While the zoning ordinance may have nothing to do directly with the problem of providing space for recreation, the fact that the zoning laws do restrict the use of private real estate and cause a division of the city into various types of districts has a bearing on the problem of recreation.

From the point of view of the economist, city planning is an attempt to prevent waste. " The comptroller of a large life insurance company estimated that the present method of

---

[1] Civic Development Department of the Chamber of Commerce of the United States, *City Planning and Zoning*, Washington, D. C., June, 1925, pp. 5, 6.

[2] Advisory Committee on Zoning of the U. S. Department of Commerce, *A Zoning Primer*, rev. ed., 1926, Government Printing Office, Washington, p. 1.

American city growth involves an annual loss of over a billion dollars." [1] The traffic engineer is interested in city planning because of its efforts to solve the problems of the routing of traffic to overcome the evils of congestion. The landscape architect thinks of the city plan as a method of beautifying the city. But for the sociologist, no one of these views is the all-absorbing one. He is interested in the city plan as it effects a redistribution of population, or as it provides better housing facilities or working conditions with their consequent effects on health, mortality and crime, or as it offers a more favorable environment for the youth, with the effects of that on delinquency, safety, health and welfare.

If it be assumed that recreation does have some relation to these last-named problems, then the bearing of city planning is significant. The sociologist is intensely interested in legislation for any measure which will affect public health, redistribution of population, crime, and general welfare. " One of its (city planning's) dominant purposes always, however, is to promote, to extend, and to make more adequate and more perfect the provisions for public recreation." [2] Inasmuch as the city plan is concerned with the problem of recreation, and recreation is a legitimate field for the student of human society, the following discussion on the legislation which looks toward the provision of adequate recreational space in the future American city is justifiable.

But before discussing the legislation it is important to ask several questions. How much recreational space does a city need, and how should that space be distributed? Many cities have either within their limits or in the metropolitan area adequate open spaces. But the more important problem is

[1] Nolen, John, *Twenty Years of City Planning Progress in the U. S.,* National Conference on City Planning, New York, 1927, 46 pp., p. 20.

[2] Nolen, John, " The Parks and Recreation Facilities in the U. S.," *Annals of the American Academy of Political and Social Sciences,* 1910, vol. xxxv, p. 227.

the one of the proper distribution of such areas. And that is the problem which the city plan aims to solve. The Civic Development Department of the United States Chamber of Commerce [1] is authority for the statement that " Probably less than one per cent of American playgrounds have been carefully planned. . . . If we are to have proper playground systems, properly coordinated and allowing for efficient use, we must first give attention to the matter of planning." For example, New York City has in its metropolitan area ample open spaces for recreational purposes, but they are not distributed in such a way as to provide sufficient play spaces in points of densest concentration of population.

That such a condition as this may be remedied in the future American city, the city planners consider as the necessary initial step in their program the adoption by all municipalities of a comprehensive city plan. This plan should show the areas to be set aside for recreation. In so far as legislation is concerned, the states in thirty instances have passed general city-planning enabling acts giving to cities powers to adopt and carry into effect comprehensive plans. These laws follow in general outlines the Standard City Planning Enabling Act prepared by the Advisory Committee on City Planning and Zoning of the United States Department of Commerce. But before any individual city's plan as it relates to recreational areas can be drafted, it must be determined how much space is needed and the distribution of that space so as to serve present and future populations. Consequently there has been considerable work done in recent years to arrive at standards for the extent and distribution of such areas.

The first question, as to how much play space a city needs, has been answered variously, as : [2]

[1] Civic Development Department of the Chamber of Commerce of the U. S., *Playgrounds*, Washington, D. C., 1922, 13 pp.

[2] Curtis, H. S., " Can America Afford an Adequate System of Playgrounds? ", *American City*, New York, July, 1927, p. 65. (*See p. 31, foot.*)

Ten acres for every thousand children.

Five acres for every thousand persons.

Forty-three square feet per child, or about one acre for every thousand children.

Thirty square feet per child, or less than one acre for every thousand children.

Ten per cent of the city's gross acreage.

Five per cent of the city's gross acreage.

But such attempts to arrive at a fixed standard do not take into account two important factors, namely, the changing population density and the varying character of the recreation of children at different ages. In the case of the former, what might have been a wholly inadequate area on the lower east side of Manhattan ten years ago might today be sufficient space because of population mobility. In the case of the latter, where one acre per thousand children in the population of an area might be sufficient for sand boxes, swings and other apparatus for small children, such an area would be absolutely inadequate for older children, with whom group games are the usual form of play.

In any attempt to arrive at standards for play areas, especially in regard to children, these factors must be taken into account: the density of the population; the number of children who will play and how they are distributed in age groups; the distance which the individual will travel to a play area, dependent upon the age of the child; and the number of children who will use the play area at any one time: the "light" load and the "peak" load. With these factors in mind, studies have been made in a given neighbor-

National Playing Fields Association—London, report to be presented at first annual regular meeting for period July 8, 1925 to April 12, 1927.

"Planning and Administration of a Modern City's Recreation," *American City*, New York, October, 1927, p. 475.

Chambers, C. E., "The Distribution of Park Areas," *Parks and Recreation*, Rockford, Ill., Nov.-Dec., 1926, pp. 119 *et seq.*

hood to determine how much space is needed for play and how much is actually provided. Rowland Haynes [1] applied these four factors to a neighborhood in New York City and found that by means of the present space in use together with all the available space in the section that was suited for use, seventy-nine per cent of the need could be met. The Department of Recreation of the Russell Sage Foundation has been carrying on studies in measuring the relation between the space needed for recreation in the boroughs of New York City and that actually available. [2] Taking a more or less arbitrary standard of one hundred square feet of space for each child and taking into account the number of children, the boroughs were divided into districts of approximately equal size. The purpose of the division of the territory into small districts was to map out what might be termed natural play areas. A measure of play-space adequacy in terms of per cent was secured by relating the factors mentioned above,—population, amount of space needed per child, number of children who would play and distance they would travel,—to the space actually available.

Apart from such objective approaches to the problem of standards, there have been many suggestions made as to standards growing out of the experiences of recreation leaders. Henry V. Hubbard [3] makes these suggestions regarding the distribution of parks and play areas:

[1] Haynes, Rowland, "How Much Playground Space does a City Need?" *American City Pamphlet No. 158*, New York, 7 pp.

[2] Hanmer, Lee F., *Public Recreation, A Study of Parks, Playgrounds and Other Outdoor Recreation Facilities, Regional Survey*, vol. v., *Regional Plan of New York and Its Environs*, New York, 1928, 256 pp.

[3] Hubbard, Henry V., *Parks and Playgrounds—American Experience as to Their Requirements and Distribution as Elements in the City Plan*, 1924, 25 pp. Revised from paper given before the American National Conference on City Planning, for presentation at the International Town Planning Conference, Amsterdam, 1924.

Play Lots — one in each block.

Neighborhood Playgrounds — one every half-mile apart, serving the children within a radius of one-quarter mile and the size of an average block.

District Playgrounds — located every mile, serving the children of over twelve years, and having an effective radius of one-half mile.

" Intown Parks " — located by convenience and use.

Landscape Park and Reservation — located with relation to the cost of the land and the means of transportation, having an effective radius co-extensive with the city.

A committee report [1] to the Recreation Congress held at Springfield, Illinois, in 1923 made these recommendations as to standards:

1. *Play Lots,* for children under five years, from six to ten thousand square feet in size, to be located near the center of every one hundred children and to be reached without the necessity of crossing the street.

2. *Neighborhood Playgrounds,* for children six to fourteen years of age, four to ten acres in size, and having a radius of effectiveness of one-half mile.

3. *District Playgrounds,* for children twelve years and up, ten to twenty-four acres in size, with a radius of one-half to one mile and one for every eight to twelve thousand population.

4. *Recreation Park,* a tract of from one hundred to two hundred and fifty acres, located on the outskirts of the city.

5. *Reservation,* a public area owned by the state, county, city or federal government.

This Congress was unanimous in agreement on the proposal

[1] Report of a Committee to the Recreation Congress—Springfield, Ill., October 11, 1923, *Recreational Problems in City Planning.*

that all playgrounds for children under eleven or twelve years of age should be adjacent to the public elementary school, and that municipal playgrounds for children over eleven or twelve years be provided in connection with the junior and senior high schools. To that end it was recommended that there should be a minimum of eight acres of play space connected with every elementary school; of ten to twenty acres with the intermediate school, and twenty to forty acres with the high school.

These examples of the suggestions that have been made and the objective studies that have been projected should reveal that there is far from a general consensus of opinion on the vexed question of standards. There is need for further objective approaches to the problem, taking into account all of the factors in the situation. However, sufficient information is available to serve as a guide to the city planner in making provision for recreational areas to meet the present and future needs of the city, both as to extent and distribution. This much is certain, viz., that the play spaces in the congested sections of our large cities are not adequate. To avoid the repetition of such a situation in the future, it is necessary to plan for recreation spaces in areas which are now unbuilt but which some day will form part of the city's growth. A difficulty which is met with at once in any such planning is the fact that one can only conjecture as to possible future needs for such areas and the density of population in sections that are now unbuilt. Of course, the planner has a guide in the past development of the city. The difficulty is not insuperable when one considers the intelligence and foresight with which L'Enfant laid out the city of Washington.

To be sure, there is another difficulty and a more serious one in making provision for recreation in sections of the city as yet undeveloped. If the public owned the land over which the city was likely to spread, it would be an easy matter for the city government to follow the advice of the planners. But such is not the case. New developments which are later added to the city are first projected by private real-estate operators. The only legal powers which the city can exercise are those granted to the city-planning commissions by the state laws. After the state has passed a city-planning enabling act, it is the usual practice for a municipality to appoint a city-planning commission. This commission then calls in an engineer to draw up a comprehensive plan for the entire metropolitan area. Among the powers given to this commission is that of requiring a real-estate subdivider to have the plat of his subdivision submitted to it for approval. If the plat conforms to the city plan in such matters as streets and thoroughfares, the commission will approve it; otherwise the commission will suggest changes to make it conform to the city plan, and on the failure of the subdivider to accept the suggestions, it can withhold approval and registration of the plat.

But can the city-planning commission under its grant of powers from the state legislature compel the subdivider to set aside areas for recreational purposes? Granting that it has been generally agreed that eight to twelve per cent of the area of new subdivisions outside of street space [1] should be devoted to play parks, what legal measures are there which can enforce such a provision? Minnesota had a law passed in 1885 and applicable to St. Paul, requiring that real-estate men making a plat of twenty acres or more had to set aside one-twentieth of it for a public park. The experience of the city under this law was that real-estate operators " having more than twenty acres to plat made two plats or three if necessary and filed them at different periods in order to get

[1] Bassett, Edward M., "Legislation for Parks and Recreation Spaces," paper read before the Recreation Congress, Atlantic City, Oct. 18, 1924.

away from the park dedication clause." [1]   The law, having become of no effect, was repealed.   With regard to subsequent legislation, Mr. Herrold continues:

Our platting laws adopted in 1887 are rather crude and meager, but we have been able to do a great many things by persuasion, and since the adoption of our zoning ordinance we can, of course, refuse any plat where the lots do not give the area required under the zoning ordinance for the various zones.

The State of Washington tried five times, in 1907, 1911, 1923, 1925 and 1926, but without success, to have a law enacted requiring any plat of land of ten acres or more, within or without the city limits, to have one-tenth of the area, after deducting the land required for streets and alleys, set aside for a public place, park, common or playground. In one of the attempts, the bill passed both houses of the legislature but was vetoed by the governor.   The objection raised to this and other legislation along the same line was that it involved a confiscation of property without due process of law.   Illinois in 1917 and Pennsylvania in 1923 attempted similar legislation, but both failed of enactment. Of two measures introduced in Illinois, one provided for the compulsory dedication of one-tenth of plats of ten acres or more, the other provided for dedication of one-twentieth of the area or the payment into the city treasury for park purposes of a sum equal to one-twentieth of the value of all the property in the subdivision.   The Pennsylvania proposal provided for an area of at least ten thousand square feet in every subdivision of four acres or more, the same to be deeded to the board of school directors of the district in which the subdivision was located.

The only state legislation now on the statute books requir-

[1] Extract from letter of George H. Herrold, Managing Director of City Planning, Plat Commission of Ramsey County, Minnesota, to the author, Nov. 17, 1927.

ing the dedication of a specific amount of land in new sub-divisions for recreational purposes is the Montana law, which reads as follows: [1]

What plat must contain — The plat must show as follows:

9. For the purpose of promoting the public comfort, welfare and safety, such plat and survey must show that at least one-ninth of the platted area, exclusive of streets, alleys, avenues and highways, is forever dedicated to the public for parks and play-grounds; the one-half of such area so dedicated to the public for parks and playgrounds may be distributed in small lots of not less than one block in area through the different parts of the area platted; and the one-half shall be consecrated into larger parks on the outer edge of the area so platted. The board of county commissioners of the county, or the council of the city or town, is hereby authorized to suggest suitable places for such parks and playgrounds, and for good cause shown may make an order in the proceedings of such body (to be indorsed and certified on said plat), diminishing the amount of such area herein required to be dedicated as public parks and playgrounds to not less than one-twelfth thereof, exclusive of streets, alleys, avenues, and highways; provided, that where such platted area consists of a tract of land containing less than twenty acres, such board of county commissioners of the county, or the council of the city or town, may make an order in the proceedings of such body, to be endorsed and certified on said plat, that no park or playground be set aside or dedicated.

This law offers the same inducement to evasion as the one in Minnesota mentioned above, namely, the temptation to realtors to plat their subdivisions in less than twenty acres. Aside from this law and the New York law of 1926 which will be considered later, the states have not gone further than to give city-planning commissions general powers over the approval of plats.

[1] *Revised Codes of Montana for 1921*, ch. 41, sec. 4981.

Under these general grants of powers, however, some municipalities have taken very definite action with regard to requiring the dedication of play areas in new plats:

Bluefield, West Virginia — Not less than five per cent of the area of all plats shall be dedicated by the owner for park and playground purposes except in the case of a very small area.[1]

Kenosha, Wisconsin — The City Plan Commission, where possible, will require the owner to dedicate for public purposes, such as parks, playgrounds and school sites, an area not more than five (5) per cent of the total area of the tract of land proposed to be platted, except where in the opinion of such Commission five (5) per cent of the area is too small for parks, playgrounds and school sites when no public dedication of said tract shall be required. The five (5) per cent hereinbefore referred to shall be exclusive of any area of said tract dedicated for streets and alleys.[2]

Lake Bluff, Illinois — In subdividing property, due consideration shall be given to the provision of suitable sites for parks, playgrounds and schools.[3]

Detroit, Michigan — In residential allotments, the Commission may request the allotter to dedicate for playgrounds or parks an area which it deems adequate for children and residents of the allotment.[4]

Memphis, Tennessee — In subdividing property, due consideration shall be given to the dedication of suitable sites for schools, parks and playgrounds. Such provision should be indicated on the preliminary plan in order that it may be determined when and in what manner such areas will be dedicated to the city.[5]

[1] Requirements for City Plats, adopted by the City Planning Commission, July 3, 1923.

[2] Land Subdivision Rules adopted May 20, 1924, Rule 9, sec. D.

[3] Subdivision Ordinance, adopted Jan. 8, 1924, pt. 2, sec. C.

[4] Platting Regulations of the City Plan Commission, June, 1921.

[5] Land Subdivision Rules, published as Appendix G of the Final Report of the Memphis City Plan Commission, 1924, sec. ii.

Los Angeles County, California — While not officially required, the reservation of from five to ten per cent of large subdivisions for public use is strongly urged, and has frequently been demonstrated to be an economically sound provision.[1]

St. Louis, Missouri — In subdividing property, due consideration should be given to the dedication of suitable property for sites for schools, parks and playgrounds. Such provision should be indicated on the preliminary plan in order that it may be determined when and in what manner such parks and playgrounds will be received for dedication by the city.[2]

In a word, then, it may be said that the states have done little to require that plats of new subdivisions shall provide as a condition of their approval the setting aside of a certain percent of the land for recreational purposes. Some city-planning commissions have been bold enough to make such a requirement and have " gotten away with it ". Whether they are within the powers granted by the state enabling act is a question which has not been tested by the courts. The City Planning Commission of Akron, Ohio, in its rules, adopted 1920, required the allotter to dedicate such land as the commission might deem adequate for the future recreational needs of the new community. However, this provision was in force only until 1923. In that year, the state passed a new law providing that the dedication of property for other than street purposes should not be made a condition of approval of the plat.

The New York State Laws passed in 1926 [3] offer one solution to the problem of securing in advance play-parks in unbuilt areas. These laws make the usual provisions for the

[1] General Requirements for the Subdivision of Land, Los Angeles County Regional Planning Commission, Los Angeles, January, 1927.

[2] Annual Reports for 1921 and 1922 and Rules for Land Subdivision, City Planning Commission, St. Louis, Appendix sec x, adopted Nov. 16, 1921.

[3] *Laws of New York*, 1926, chs. 690 and 719.

creation of a planning board, the adoption of a plan, and the powers of approving plats. They are unusual in that they require that the plats shall show, in addition to proposed streets and highways, a park or parks suitably located for playground or other recreational purposes. Paragraph 33 of the law reads:

Before the approval by the planning board of a plat showing a new street or highway, such plat shall also in proper cases show a park or parks suitably located for playground or other recreational purposes. In approving such plats the planning board shall require that the streets and highways shall be of sufficient width and suitably located to accommodate the prospective traffic and to afford adequate light, air and access of fire-fighting equipment to buildings, and to be co-ordinated so as to compose a convenient system; that the land shown on such plats shall be provided with proper sanitary and drainage conditions; and that the parks shall be of reasonable size for neighborhood playgrounds or other recreational uses. In making such determination regarding streets, highways and parks, the planning board shall take into consideration the prospective character of the development, whether dense residence, business or industrial.

This would seem to be a wiser provision than one of requiring the dedication of a fixed per cent of the land in view of the fact that different subdivisions will have different needs with regard to recreation. Leaving to the planning board the determination of the area to be devoted to such use may seem a bit arbitrary, and yet the subdivider by the provisions of the act is not left without recourse. Part of section 36 of the Act provides:

Where the enforcement of the provisions of this section would entail practical difficulty or unnecessary hardship, and where the circumstances of the case do not require the structure to be related to existing or proposed streets or highways, the applicant for such permit may appeal from the decision of the administrative officer having charge of the issue of permits to the board of appeals or other similar board in any city which established a board having power to make variances or exceptions in zoning regulations, and the same provisions are hereby applied to such appeals and to such board as are provided in cases of appeals on zoning regulations.

The distinctions between this and other state laws are obvious. It does not make the dedication of play areas compulsory. It gives the subdivider an opportunity to defend himself before a board of appeals. It enables the owner to make up for the land he gives for recreation by permitting certain changes in street width, permitting building in the bed of mapped streets, and other zoning changes. In fact, it gives to the body having to do with zoning regulations the power to make sufficient concessions from the zoning restrictions applicable to the plat to allow the subdivider to make up altogether for the land he devotes to play space.

Under the grant of powers made in these laws, certain municipalities in New York State have adopted local ordinances. The city of Jamestown is an example. The ordinance adopted by the city council August 9, 1926 calls for the preparation of an official map, and the creation of a planning commission together with the local machinery to carry into effect the provisions of the state law. On its creation, the City Planning Commission adopted certain rules, one of which reads: "A minimum dedication for park purposes of 10 per cent of the area of the subdivision may be required." [1]

It remains to be seen whether the flexibility given to the new law by the provision whereby the board of appeals may set aside zoning restrictions in behalf of the securing of parks and playgrounds is going to operate as a measure of

[1] Rules Governing the Platting and Submission of New Subdivisions to the City Planning Commission, Jamestown, N. Y., 1927, sec. 23: a.

strength or of weakness in this new legislation. The superiority of the New York law over other state laws lies just here in the powers given to the board of appeals to make concessions in zoning regulations. It is to be expected that the working out of this law will lead, in the beginning, to certain abuses and the grant of special favors to certain individuals. And this is the most poignant criticism which has been made of this law. But just as soon as a body of precedent and decisions has been built up, the board of appeals will undoubtedly prove to be an element of strength in zoning procedures.

Apart from the legislative action, much has been done by the voluntary cooperation of the real-estate subdivider to provide recreational areas in the future development of the American city. The campaign of publicity being carried on by the Playground and Recreation Association of America and the Harmon Foundation together with the cooperation of the National Association of Real Estate Boards, seems to be convincing the real-estate fraternity that, if for no other reason, self-interest would dictate the setting aside of play areas. If William E. Harmon[1] and J. C. Nichols[2] are correct, the five per cent or ten per cent set aside for recreational purposes is not lost but is more than made up for in the enhanced value of the remaining acreage. However, there is a larger interest involved, namely, the public welfare. And the real-estate operators are cooperating with the city planners in realizing that larger interest. At the National Conference on City Planning, held in Washington, D. C., June, 1927, the joint committee on subdivision control of the

---

[1] Harmon, William E., "A Message from William E. Harmon," Playground and Recreation Association of America, New York, *Bulletin No. 198*, 12 pp.

[2] Nichols, J. C., *Real Estate Subdivisions, the Best Manner of Handling Them*, American Civic Association, 1912, 15 pp.

National Association of Real Estate Boards and the American City Planning Institute made this suggestion as part of its report:[1]

7. The general requirements for principal public parks and recreational spaces and sites for public buildings should be included as part of the master plan. Where a landowner has submitted a plat of his land and authorities have designated in it such a principal park, recreation space or public building site as part of the master plan, the municipality should take prompt steps to acquire such land, or failing to do so, should act upon the plat, so that the owner can make use of his property. The subdivider should be encouraged to provide small private recreational parks.

The cooperation of state real-estate associations in this movement is evidenced from the following extracts:

Dedication of a portion of new subdivisions for parks, playground and community recreation purposes is approved by the Massachusetts Association of Real Estate Boards in a resolution passed by its board of directors.[2]

Be it Resolved, that the Michigan Real Estate Association hereby expresses its opinion that subdividers of new tracts have it within their power to exhibit real statesmanship and to perform a splendid public service by setting aside portions of their properties for perpetual community use as parks and playgrounds while at the same time enhancing the attractiveness of their area without lessening the returns from sales.

We urge on all Realtors serious consideration of this policy and application thereof wherever possible.[3]

What some of the realtors are doing voluntarily to meet

[1] " Planners and Realtors Cooperate in Subdivision Control," *American City*, July, 1927, p. 34.

[2] *American City*, Sept., 1927, p. 338.

[3] *National Real Estate Journal*, Oct. 3, 1927, p. 60.

this problem will be apparent from a few selected illustrations. At Sunnyside, in the Borough of Queens, New York City, a development has been made by the City Housing Corporation, providing homes for 1200 families, laid out in such a way that only thirty per cent of the blocks are built upon, leaving space for trees, gardens, tennis courts and an interior playground.[1] In the St. Francis Wood Subdivision in San Francisco, from eight to ten per cent is reserved for play space; of eighteen subdivisions in Greensboro, North Carolina, there is an average of 14.6 per cent set aside for this purpose; the Bayonne Housing Corporation of Bayonne, New Jersey, has devoted 22.4 per cent to the public for playground purposes; of the Red Acres Subdivision in Memphis, Tennessee, 44.5 per cent is reserved for recreation and other public uses.[2] Even golf courses are being laid out in new subdivisions.[3] The Puget Mill Company of Seattle, Washington, laid out a golf course in a two-hundred-acre subdivision; in Kansas City, J. C. Nichols has laid out four links in his subdivisions.

These examples are merely illustrative of what realtors are doing throughout the country to meet the problem voluntarily. A program of education and promotion is being carried on at the present time by Mr. H. C. Stone and the Playground and Recreation Association of America to convince realty men that the making of such provisions for the future needs of great cities is an investment which pays in every way. " Up to the present time the Association has record of nearly 200 real-estate developments where pro-

[1] "Sunnyside—An Experiment in City Housing," *Survey*, Nov. 15, 1924, p. 189.

[2] Wood, M. Travis, " Subdividing for Play," *American City*, August, 1927, pp. 140-146.

[3] " Golf Courses in Subdivisions," *National Real Estate Journal*, August 23, 1926, pp. 52, 53.

vision has been made for play and recreation areas." [1] Such a statement bears witness to the success of this campaign of publicity.

The problems, however, awaiting solution in connection with this whole question are by no means simple. If a realtor exercises his constitutional right to withhold dedication of his plat and decides to sell by metes and bounds, he may choose to set aside play areas and develop them as a selling point in disposing of his lots. But after the subdivision has been disposed of, he feels no further obligation to pay for the expense of maintaining such areas. Then the question of maintenance falls either upon the property owners or the city government if the tract has been entered. In the Sunnyside development mentioned above, the deeds to the properties call for the cooperation of the owners of the properties in an association for the purpose of maintaining the play areas.

Still another situation may arise, and has arisen. A subdivider may set aside a portion of his plat for permanent recreation grounds and may have the same entered upon the city plan and dedicated in perpetuity to the city. But suppose, as has happened, the subdivision does not develop rapidly and the need for the area is not immediately experienced. There is no law compelling such municipality to maintain the property and the city officials allow the land to grow in weeds and become a nuisance. If in the future there are going to be state laws requiring the dedication of some part of every new subdivision for park and recreational purposes, or if, in the absence of such laws, the realtors are willing to set aside areas for such purposes, then it would seem as though there ought to be some provision for compelling the municipal governments to maintain such areas.

[1] Playground and Recreation Association of America, " Play Space," *Bulletin # 1670*, July 1, 1927.

Such legal provision might stipulate that in the absence of such maintenance, the title to such property would revert to the realtor.

BIBLIOGRAPHY

Bassett, Edward M., *Recent New York Legislation for the Planning of Unbuilt Areas*, Regional Plan of New York and its Environs, 1926, 30 pp.

Culham, Gordon J. and Mayer, Frederick M., Jr., "The Seasonable Acquisition of Parks and Other Public Open Spaces," *Landscape Architecture*, vol. xv, 1924-5, pp. 16-29.

Ford, George B., *What Planning Has Done for Cities*, National Conference on City Planning, 1924, 21 pp.

Kimball, Theodora, *Manual of Information on City Planning and Zoning*, Harvard University Press, 1923, 188 pp.

Lommel, G. E. and Bates, F. G., "A City Planning Primer," *Bull. No. 11*, Engineering Extension Service, Purdue University, July, 1925, 32 pp.

Nolen, John, *City Planning*, D. Appleton and Co., 1916, 447 pp.

Rex, Frederick, *Report on State Laws and Municipal Ordinances providing that Subdivisions of Large Tracts of Land Shall Not be Accepted, Approved or Recorded by Public Officials Unless in Such Subdivisions Reservations are Made for Public Parks, Playgrounds and Similar Recreational Purposes*, Municipal Reference Library, Chicago, 1926, 13 pp. mim.

Williams, Frank B., *The Law of City Planning and Zoning*, The Macmillan Co., 1922, 738 pp.

CHAPTER II

THE MUNICIPALITY AS THE UNIT IN CONDUCTING A PROGRAM OF RECREATION

City planning in this country has just cast off its swaddling clothes. The theorizing period is giving way to the stage of working out the ideas into concrete realities. Enough data are now available for new cities to be built to meet new needs. The plans laid out for Radburn, New Jersey, to meet the needs of the present motor age; [1] the development of Mariemont, Ohio, as a model community with " its own stores, parks, lagoons, community centre, athletic field, school, inn and church "; [2] these are examples of the dreams of city planners come true. It is easier, of course, to realize such ideals in cities which are to be built than to remake cities already shaped. The latter problem does come in for considerable attention, however, and the suggestions growing out of the studies made by the Regional Plan of New York and Its Environs are efforts not only to control the future development of that city but also to remold its present condition.

The comparative infancy of city planning as a concrete science together with the lack of agreement among recreation leaders as to the recreation needs of a city may account for the inadequacy of legislation as revealed in the preceding chapter. Whether the future legislation is to follow the

[1] Chase, Stuart, "A Suburban Garden City for the Motor Age," *New York Times*, June 24, 1928.

[2] "Mariemont Aims to Set Example as Utopian City," *New York Times*, Oct. 20, 1927.

New York law remains to be seen.   It may be that the courts will give a broad interpretation to the powers of the city-planning commissions created under the existing state-enabling acts.   It is almost too much to expect that the real-estate operators will meet the entire need voluntarily.

Although the legislation to provide recreation areas in the future developments of the city has been inadequate, there has been no lack of legislation for public outdoor recreation by governmental agencies.   The logical approach to the analysis of such legislation would be to begin with the national government, continue with the state governments and end with the local units.   This would be the reasonable method of attack in view of the fact that the local unit has been regarded as the creation of the state legislature, deriving its powers from that body.   But up to this time, at least, the conduct of recreation has been chiefly a local concern. Neither in the federal nor in the state governmental machinery has there been created a department having to do with the whole problem of recreation.   On the contrary the municipality has been active in setting up a governmental agency to provide for, operate and control a local recreation program.

The time may well come when it will be necessary in the interests of a coordinated system to have such federal and state agencies.   The concentration of the population in cities and the present means of rapid transit, the railroad, the motor car and the airplane, have brought home to recreation leaders the importance of a nationally coordinated system of highways, transportation facilities and recreation areas.   If the opportunities for recreation are to reach all of the people, then the municipal and county areas open for such purposes must be coordinated with the state and federal parks, in one great system, joined conveniently by good highways.   The broad outlines of such a comprehensive national plan have already been conceived. Cyrus Kehr [1] and Warren H. Manning [2] have attacked the problem, but its solution is for the future.

In considering, then, what has been done by legislation in the field of public outdoor recreation, the municipality because of its importance will be taken up first. Before it is possible to make any such study something must be said with regard to the relation between the state and local government. In colonial America charters were granted by the governor or proprietor, acting in place of the crown. Hence, the early state constitutions accepted the tradition, without in many instances even writing it into their constitutions, that the right to charter cities within their borders was their privilege and power. The extent to which this privilege was carried led, notably from the middle to the end of the last century, to its abuse by the state legislatures. This abuse expressed itself not only in the vast amount of special legislation enacted by states for specific cities, but also to acts abolishing municipal corporations and even to supplanting local officials by state law.

The reaction to this misuse of power on the part of the state government came in the form of constitutional home-rule and began in Missouri in 1875. " The essence of this plan is that the city shall be permitted to draft, adopt and subsequently amend its local charter subject to the general laws of the state." [3] To be sure, such charters can only be adopted when provision has been made by an amendment to the state constitution and they can only give to cities

---

[1] Kehr, Cyrus, *A Nation Plan, A Basis for Coordinated Physical Development of the United States of America*, Oxford University Press, 1926, 210 pp.

[2] Manning, Warren H., *A National Plan Study Brief*, supplement to *Landscape Architecture* for July, 1923, 24 pp.

[3] Anderson, William, *American City Government*, Henry Holt and Co., New York, 1925, 675 pp., p. 46.

powers over local affairs. This is implied in Dillon's definition of a municipal corporation:[1] " A municipal corporation,
in its strict and proper sense, is the body politic and corporate
constituted by the incorporation of the inhabitants of a city
or town for the purposes of local government thereof."
The classic summary of the powers of municipal corporations
is: (1) those granted in express words; (2) those necessarily
implied or incident to the powers expressly granted; (3)
those essential to the declared objects and purposes of the
corporation.

Fifteen states have delegated by constitutional provision
powers of self-government to cities. But, " a city in making
its own charter may not arrogate to itself powers which the
state as a whole needs to exercise for the people as a whole."[2]
Hence the bounds within which the municipal corporation has
exclusive jurisdiction are by no means settled. " Who shall
decide," asks McBain,[3] " whether this or that specific matter
is a proper subject for regulation and control by a municipality?" And the same author answers: " It is the courts
which have been saddled with the almost impossible duty of
defining the vague and uncertain terms in which these constitutional grants have been made." The evidence of the
impossibility of defining a subject for regulation and control
by a municipal corporation is apparent from the wide diversity of interpretation put upon constitutional home-rule by
different jurisdictions. In the case of the City of Cleveland
v. Legal News Publishing Co.,[4] the question at issue was

---

[1] Dillon, John Forrest, *Commentaries on the Law of Municipal Corporations*, Little, Brown and Co., Boston, 5 vols., 5th ed., 1911, vol. i,
sec. 31, p. 18.

[2] Anderson, *op. cit.*, p. 62.

[3] McBain, H. L., *American City Progress and the Law*, Columbia
University Press, New York, 1918, 269 pp., p. 5.

[4] 110 Ohio Stat. 360. See also Tooke, C. W., *A Selection of Cases on
the Law of Municipal Corporations*, Callaghan and Co., 1926, 1335 pp.,
pp. 429, 430.

one concerning the power of the city to contract for advertising at a rate which was higher than the rate provided in a state law. The court ruled that a municipality had no right to make an agreement to have its advertising done at a rate which was in strict violation of the state statute. On the other hand the California Supreme Court went a long way toward setting forth the principle of complete local autonomy when it said : [1] " Cities organized under the municipal affairs amendment to the Constitution are entirely beyond the interference of general laws. . . . A charter provision relating to a purely municipal affair contravenes the general law pertaining to the same subject."

While it is true that fifteen states, Missouri, California, Washington, Minnesota, Colorado, Oklahoma, Oregon, Michigan, Ohio, Arizona, Texas, Nebraska, New York, Wisconsin and New Jersey, have by constitutional amendment delegated to municipal corporations within their borders powers over local affairs, there is no general agreement as to the extent of these powers. That the movement for local home-rule of the past fifty years has been a significant one cannot be gainsaid. That the state is losing its control over the cities is hardly true. Anderson puts the case very well when he says : [2]

Local charters and other local laws are being enacted more and more by the cities themselves. . . . This phase of the new tendency we shall call municipal home-rule. The state is not losing its control over cities, however, but is exercising its power less through special legislative enactments and more through state administrative departments and boards which are given broad general powers for the purpose.

This preliminary discussion was made necessary by the

[1] Storke *v.* Santa Barbara, 244 Pac. 158.
[2] Anderson, *op. cit.*, p. 59.

question as to just what powers a municipal corporation has to establish a recreation department as part of the local government. *A priori,* it would seem to be a municipal problem, pure and simple, yet there are enough legal problems involved to permit of a very liberal or a very strict interpretation. The diversity of court opinions on the extent of municipal powers under home-rule has made it possible for city attorneys to render as just, opinions both for and against the contention that their cities had the power under constitutional home-rule to establish a recreation system.

By reason, therefore, of the legal difficulties involved, in recent years twenty-one states have passed specific home-rule acts enabling municipalities to create, operate and maintain systems of public recreation. In 1915, only two of these states, Iowa and New Jersey, had such acts, and these were subsequently amended. So it may be said that the municipal government going into the field of conducting public recreation by a separate department or by a board under an existing department of the city government is a situation which belongs almost exclusively to the period which this study aims to cover. Following the method of treatment outlined in the introduction, examples of these state-enabling acts will be presented, the first showing meager, the second fuller, and the last rather broad and inclusive provisions. Then the provisions of all the acts will be analyzed graphically in a summary digest.

Connecticut — Any town, city or borough, in addition to such powers as it has under the provisions of the general statues or by any special act, shall have power to make by-laws and ordinances for the following purposes : . . . to establish, maintain and conduct parks, playgrounds, baths, swimming pools, gymnasiums, recreation places and public gardens, and to make appropriations therefor. . . .[1]

[1] *Conn. Public Acts,* 1923, ch. 284.

Massachusetts — Any city or town may acquire land and buildings within its limits by gift or purchase, or right of eminent domain, . . . or may lease the same, or may use suitable land or buildings already owned by it, for the purposes of a public playground or recreation centre, and may conduct and promote recreation, play, sport and physical education, for which admission may be charged, on such land and in such buildings, and may construct buildings on land owned and leased by it and may provide equipment for said purposes. Buildings so acquired, leased or constructed may be used also for town meetings, and, with the consent of, and subject to the conditions and terms prescribed by, the officer or board in control of the building, may be used by the municipality, or by any department thereof, or by any person, society or other organization for such other public, recreational, social or educational purposes as the said officer or board may deem proper. For the purposes aforesaid, any city or town may appropriate money, and may employ teachers, supervisors and other officers, and may fix their compensation. Except in Boston and except as to the making of appropriations, the powers conferred by this section shall be exercised by the board of park commissioners, or by the school committee, or by a playground or recreation commission appointed by the mayor or elected by the voters of the town at a town meeting, or may be distributed between the board of park commissioners, the school committee and such playground or recreational commission, or any two of them, or they may be exercised by a committee made up from any one or more members of all or any one of said boards or commissions, accordingly as the city council or the town may decide. Any municipal officer or board authorized to exercise any of the powers conferred by this section may conduct its activities on property under its control, on other public property under the control of other public officers and boards, with the consent of such officers and boards, or on private property, with the consent of the owners.[1]

West Virginia — Sec. 1. That any city, town, county, inde-

---

[1] *General Laws of Massachusetts*, 1921, ch. 45, sec. 14.

pendent school district or school district may establish and conduct a system of public recreation and playgrounds; may set apart for such use any land or buildings owned or leased by it; may acquire land, buildings, and other recreational facilities by gift, purchase, lease, condemnation, bond issue, or otherwise, and equip and conduct the same; may employ a director of recreation and assistants; may expend funds for the aforesaid purposes.

Sec. 2. The governing authorities establishing such system may conduct the same through a department or bureau of recreation, or may delegate the conduct thereof to a recreation board created by them or to a school board or to any other appropriate existing board or commission. If they shall decide to delegate the conduct to a recreation board, the board shall consist of five persons including representation from the school board, and shall be appointed by the governing body to serve for a term of five years, or until successors are appointed, except that the members of such board first appointed shall be appointed for such terms that the term of one member shall expire annually thereafter. Vacancies in such board occurring otherwise than by expiration of term shall be for the unexpired term and shall be filled in the same manner as original appointments. Members of such board shall serve without pay.

Sec. 3. Any two or more cities, towns, counties, independent school districts or school districts may jointly establish and conduct such a system of recreation and playgrounds and may exercise all the powers given by this act.

Sec. 4. Any city, town, county, independent school district, or school district may levy annually for this purpose and in the manner provided by law for other levies and in addition to all such levies, a tax not to exceed three cents on each one hundred dollars of all the real and personal property as listed for taxation.

Sec. 5. Whenever a petition signed by legal voters of any one of the above mentioned governmental divisions, equal to twenty per cent of the votes polled at the last general election, if in a county for governor, in a city or town for mayor, or council, or in a school district for members of the board of education, as the case may be, shall be filed at least thirty days prior to any general or special election in the office of the clerk or other recording officer, the authorities shall submit to the voters at the said election the question of the establishment and conduct of a system of public recreation and playgrounds. Such petition shall request the said authorities to establish and conduct a system of public recreation and playgrounds, if there be no such system, or for the maintenance of an existing recreation system, and to levy a specified tax, annually, for the maintenance thereof, provided, that such tax shall not exceed three cents on each one hundred dollars of the assessed valuation of property subject to local taxation. The aforesaid question may also be submitted at any such election by the said local authorities on their own motion, their resolution specifying the tax to be voted on. The election when ordered shall be conducted in all respects as other elections; and the ballot shall have thereon under the heading " public recreation question " the words:

> For public recreation and playgrounds
> Against public recreation and playgrounds

Sec. 6. When such proposition is adopted by a majority of the qualified voters, voting on such proposition, the governing authorities shall provide for the establishment and conduct of a system of recreation and playgrounds, shall designate the body or department to be vested with the power and duties necessary to the conduct thereof, and shall provide for the levy and collection of said tax; but such tax shall be in addition to and exclusive of all other taxes, such governmental division may levy and collect.

Sec. 7. Any governmental division can alter or repeal this special tax in the same manner in which it created this tax.

Sec. 8. The provision of this act shall not in any wise repeal, affect or limit the powers and provisions heretofore or hereafter granted to any city, town, district, county, independent school district or school district under the provisions of any charter or by any special act or acts of the legislature, to establish, maintain and conduct parks and public recreation and playgrounds.[1]

There are no norms by which to judge of the adequacy of legislation in a given state unless one were to take the law proposed by the Playground and Recreation Association of America. This law was not drafted with the idea that it was in any sense to be regarded as a model law but was meant to serve as a suggestion to legislatures considering the question of a state-enabling act and was valuable inasmuch as it had grown out of experience in instituting programs of public recreation. The West Virginia Law, quoted in full above, comes very near to being just such a law. The advantage in having a member of the school board serving on the recreation commission is obvious. The public school through its after-school and vacation playgrounds has been the greatest public agency up to this time in providing recreation, at least for the child of school age. In any program of municipal recreation, therefore, the school authorities and the public authorities should work hand in hand. It is important too that the law should include all the local governmental divisions, especially in view of the present tendency for the county to take up the whole program of recreation. The question of maintenance has been a very difficult problem. Where the law provides that the system shall be maintained by appropriation, there is great danger that this last and youngest member of the municipal governing body may be sidetracked. This is especially true in those states which set a limit to the municipality's taxing power. Where the tax limit of the municipality is, say, ten mills, plenty of opportunity to spend this revenue has been found apart from giving any of it to a new department of the government. And when the budget calls for economy, the economy has

[1] *Acts of West Virginia*, 1925, ch. 76.

been found to fall heaviest upon this department. For this reason, several state laws provide for a special tax, exclusive of and in addition to all other taxes which the city may collect, to care for this function. If an additional provision calls for the creation of a separate fund into which the revenue from this tax is to be put, it prevents the city executive from using its funds for other municipal purposes. The advantage claimed for the referendum which calls for the voters to vote not only on the question of instituting the program but also on the amount of the tax, is that it creates a public interest in recreation which might not otherwise be felt.

A copy of the law proposed by the Playground and Recreation Association of America, together with a summary digest of the provisions of the laws in the twenty-one states having these specific home-rule enabling acts, will be found in Appendix A.

It is not to be inferred from this analysis that the states which are not included among those having specific home-rule enabling acts legalizing municipal recreation have not enacted permissive legislation. By comparing this list of twenty-one states with the fifteen states having constitutional home-rule for cities, it will be observed that only four of the fifteen, i.e., Michigan, New Jersey, New York and Ohio, have adopted municipal home-rule enabling acts covering recreation. Does this mean that in the remaining eleven states (Arizona, California, Colorado, Minnesota, Missouri, Nebraska, Oklahoma, Oregon, Texas, Washington, and Wisconsin), constitutional home-rule has been interpreted to include in the charter-making powers of cities the power to establish recreation departments? It may mean just that. In states such as California and Texas, where rather broad interpretations have been placed by the courts on the powers granted under constitutional home-rule, a number of cities have included recreation departments as separate departments of their city governments in the making of their charters. But it may mean that when a city has wanted to establish a recreation system, the state has assumed the power not to exist, but has delegated the power by " special legislation ". Such legislation often takes the form of so-called " class " legislation in which the law is made applicable to a certain class of cities within the borders of the state, of which class there may be only one or two cities.   Examples of such legislation are to be found in the Nebraska Act of 1915, granting to cities of the metropolitan class power to acquire lands for parkways, parks, playgrounds, etc., or in the Minnesota Act of 1925, granting to cities of the first class of over 50,000 population power to issue bonds up to $125,000 for the purpose of acquiring and improving lands for parks, parkways, and playgrounds.   In the second place it may mean that in the absence of " special " laws or a specific home-rule enabling act or a broad interpretation of constitutional home-rule, the city within one of these eleven states has entrusted the conduct of recreation to some other department of the city government, such as the Department of Parks and Public Property, Department of Public Welfare, or some other division.

There remain to be considered the provisions made by state legislatures for municipal recreation in those states which are not included in the two groups mentioned above, namely, those having neither constitutional home-rule nor a specific home-rule enabling act.   It would be unfair to this group of states to say that they are more blameworthy in passing a large amount of "special" legislation than the states belonging to the former groups.   It is true that in Delaware in 1925, twenty-four out of 272 chapters of the laws had to do with legislation for specific municipalities.   And an even worse situation is to be found in Maryland.   But no better a situation exists in Massachusetts, where in 1926, 176 out of 398 chapters of the laws have to do either wholly or in part with legislation for specific towns or cities. The author has felt it not germane to the analysis of legislation for public outdoor recreation to attempt, were it possible, to make a digest of the " special " legislation covering this subject. But while omitting the " special " legislation in the sixteen remaining states, it will be advisable to include examples of laws of a general nature making provision for municipal recreation, as passed by these states.

Maine — Any city or town, containing more than one thousand inhabitants, upon petition in writing signed by at least thirty of its tax-paying citizens, directed to the municipal officers, describing the land to be taken as hereinafter provided, and the names of the owners thereof so far as they are known, may, at a meeting of such town, or the city council, direct such municipal officers to take suitable lands for public parks, squares, playgrounds, buildings for municipal purposes, or a public library building; and thereupon such officers may take such land for such purposes, but not without consent of the owner, if at the time of filing such petition, with such officers, or in the office of the clerk of such town or city, such land is occupied by dwelling house wherein the owner or his family reside.[1]

Montana — All cities or towns incorporated under the laws of the state of Montana, in addition to other powers conferred upon them, may, in their discretion, construct, establish, maintain, and operate swimming pools, skating-rinks, and playgrounds within said cities or towns, and to defray the cost and expense of constructing, establishing, maintaining, and operating the same from the park funds of said city or town.[2]

North Dakota — The board of city commissioners or the city council of any city shall have the power to submit to a vote of the electors at any general or special election propositions for

[1] *Laws of Maine*, 1925, ch. 97.
[2] *Revised Codes of Montana*, 1921, sec. 5166.

the issuing of bonds for the erection of a municipal auditorium, armory, the erection of a joint auditorium and armory, public playgrounds, a public gymnasium, public baths, or other public places of amusement or entertainment, and for the purchase of suitable sites for such erection or purpose; and in case a majority of the electors voting on any such proposition vote for the same at any regular election, or at any special election called for that purpose, it shall be the duty of the board of city commissioners, or of the city council and mayor of any city, forthwith to issue bonds and proceed to carry out such proposition so submitted.[1]

Wyoming — The town council of any such town, in its corporate capacity, shall have the following powers: To establish and maintain or to assist in establishing and maintaining Community Centers and Children's Playgrounds for the benefit of the inhabitants thereof, and to make appropriations for the purpose out of the general fund of such city or town.[2]

Seven hundred and ninety cities reported maintaining community recreation programs under leadership in 1926.[3] It would be almost an impossibility to collect all of the local ordinances and charter provisions by which these cities provide the legal basis for such programs. Of this number, however, 275 reported that their recreational systems were maintained by private organizations, and as such, these do not come within the compass of this discussion. But even to gather together the local laws covering the remaining 515 would be about an equal impossibility. Happily there is considerable uniformity among these ordinances and charter provisions, so that by presenting a typical one in each of the most important categories, together with a summary digest of the provisions in cities of various sizes, it will be possible to obtain an adequate picture of what provisions the city governments are making for public outdoor recreation.

[1] *Compiled Laws of North Dakota*, vol. i, art. 15, sec. 4016.
[2] *Session Laws of Wyoming*, 1921, ch. x.
[3] *The Playground, Year Book*, April, 1927.

From the point of view of administration, there is wide divergence among these laws. By far the largest number of them vest the managing authority of the city's recreation system in either the Park Board, the School Board, or a Recreation Department. The Park Board is as old as the city government itself and has grown out of the powers delegated in many states to municipal corporations to create public parks. For example, Florida gives to cities and towns the power and authority " to lay off such parks, as may seem necessary and expedient for the public health or interest "; [1] Alabama has among its delegation of powers one which reads: " The council . . . . may establish, lay out and improve public grounds, parks and boulevards "; [2] Connecticut makes the following provision: " Any town, borough or fire district may lay out and improve any lands belonging to it, not located in any incorporated city, for a public square, common or park, and may purchase any land within its limits for that purpose." [3]

Because the Park Board is an old existing arm of the government, Wirth would maintain [4] that here is the agency ready at hand to take over the new function of recreation in all of its aspects, i.e., parks, playgrounds, athletic fields, swimming pools, public bathing beaches, gymnasiums, golf courses, summer camps, etc. But there are those who find in its very age a most powerful argument to raise against it. The Park Board has not in many quarters outlived the traditional notion concerning parks. In too many places, parks exist only to be looked at, to be beautified by shrubbery,

[1] *Revised General Statutes of Florida*, 1920, sec. 1851.

[2] *Code of Alabama*, 1923, vol. i, sec. 2018.

[3] *General Statutes of Connecticut*, revision of 1918, sec. 444.

[4] Wirth, Theodore, " Is Park Department the Logical Branch of City Government to Conduct Municipal Recreation Program? ", *Parks and Recreation*, vol. x, Nov.-Dec., 1926, pp. 141-144.

and be well adorned with signs of " Keep Off The Grass ". For that reason, the advocates of play areas have been insisting on the creation of a separate department of the city government, to be known as the Recreation Department or Commission.

There is a third agency, which was mentioned above and which must be taken into consideration in the discussion of administration, and that is the School Board. It must not be forgotten that for the children of school age, the school is the largest contributor to such children's recreational needs. During the summer of 1928, the Board of Education of the City of New York conducted supervised play on 381 playgrounds, as compared with 94 conducted by the other governmental agencies combined. Because of its importance in any program of public recreation, and because of the constant overlapping of agencies, Jay B. Nash is of the opinion [1] that the two agencies, viz, the recreation department of the city government and the board of education, should combine their work and cooperate in the employment of one superintendent of recreation.

Aside from the difference in administration, the local laws differ in other respects. Over what types of recreation does the governing body have control? Is it given general supervision over play and recreation, or is there a specific enumeration made of the types of activity over which the commission has authority? Is the system maintained by an appropriation out of the city treasury, or by means of an annual tax? If the latter, is there provision for the tax to be voted by the electors? Is power granted to conduct recreational activities on property under the park department, school board or other agencies? Is the city permitted to supervise recreational activities within and without the city limits? The Play-

---

[1] Nash, Jay B., *The Organization and Administration of Playgrounds and Recreation*, A. S. Barnes and Co., New York, 1927, 547 pp., ch. ix.

ground and Recreation Association of America has suggested an ordinance embodying the making of adequate provisions. A copy of this ordinance, together with a summary digest of the provisions of ordinances and charter provisions in sixty cities, will be found in Appendix A.

Following the method pursued with regard to the state legislation covering specific enabling acts, several examples of municipal laws are given below, illustrating different degrees of provisions, from meager to full.

Grand Rapids, Mich. — Subject to the supervision and control of the City Manager in all matters, the Director of Public Welfare shall have general supervision, management and control of all hospitals and all health, recreational, charitable, reformatory and correctional institutions and agencies belonging to or conducted by the City; of all parks belonging to or controlled by the City, of playgrounds and cemeteries; of all trees, plants, shrubbery and lawns in the streets and highways of the City.[1]

Minneapolis, Minn. — The director of parks shall manage and control all parks, parkways, boulevards, playgrounds, public gymnasiums, public bath houses, boat houses, bathing beaches, and social centers of the city, and have the management and supervision of all recreational facilities and activities developed or supported by the city government other than those for and in connection with the public schools; but nothing in this charter shall preclude any arrangement approved by the school and library boards whereby any or all of the recreational facilities of the public schools may be placed under the management and control of the director of parks.[2]

Fall River, Mass. — Section 1. A Recreation Commission shall be established in the City of Fall River under the provisions of the General Acts of 1919, Chapter 217. Said Commission shall be composed of seven members appointed in the following

[1] City Charter, adopted 1916, am. 1922.

[2] City Charter, adopted, 1925.

manner: Five members, at least two of whom shall be women, shall be appointed by the Mayor for terms of five years until their successors are appointed, except that the members of said commission first appointed shall be appointed for such terms that the term of one member shall expire annually thereafter; two other members, representatives of the School Committee and of the Park Commission, respectively, shall be appointed by their respective boards to serve for terms of one year. Vacancies in said Commission occurring otherwise than by expiration of term shall be for the unexpired term and shall be filled in the same manner as the original appointments. The members of said Commission shall serve without compensation.

Section 2. Said Commission shall have the dispensing of all funds appropriated for the maintenance and operation of its work. It shall be the duty of said Commission to organize, arrange and supervise whatever provisions are made by the City for recreation in its broadest sense, including playgrounds, playfields, indoor and outdoor centers, or related recreational activities.

Section 3. The commission shall have the power to employ a superintendent of recreation and such assistants, supervisors, play leaders, teachers, directors, engineers and other employees as may be deemed necessary for the efficient administration and development of a public recreation system, as authorized by said Recreation Commission, and provided for in its budget.

Section 4. Said Commisison shall render such regular and special reports as it may deem necessary, and as may be required by the Mayor and Board of Aldermen. It shall prepare annually suggestions to the Mayor for the budget for the year to come, together with a report covering the work and service of the closing year.[1]

Fort Worth, Texas — Section 1. There shall be a Public Recreation Board consisting of five members.

Section 2. The members of the Public Recreation Board shall be appointed by the Mayor with the advice and approval of the

---

[1] Ordinance, adopted 1924.

City Commissioners. No person shall be eligible to appointment who is not a citizen of the United States and a resident of the city. At least two of the members of the Board shall be women.

Section 3. The term of office of the members of the Public Recreation Board shall, subject to the provisions relative to removal, be five years. The members of the first Board existing hereunder shall be appointed within sixty days after the adoption of this amendment as a part of the City Charter of the City of Fort Worth and shall be appointed for the term of one year, two years, three years, four years and five years respectively, and annually thereafter one member shall be appointed for the term of five years. Members of the Board shall serve without compensation.

Section 4. Members of the Board shall be subject to removal from office by the Mayor and only after a public hearing upon charges publicly made. Any vacancy in office shall be filled by the Mayor by and with the advice and approval of the City Commissioners.

Section 5. The Board of Public Recreation shall have power and authority to equip, operate, supervise and maintain playgrounds, athletic fields, swimming centers, indoor recreation centers, municipal camps, or other recreational facilities on or in any public grounds or buildings, whether within or without the city, which the City Commission may from time to time provide, acquire, authorize, offer, designate or set apart for such use; it shall have power, with the consent of the School Board, to organize and conduct play and recreation activities on grounds and in buildings under the control of the School Board provided that nothing in this section be construed to abridge the powers of the School Board to refuse the use of any of its grounds or buildings; it shall have the power to take charge of and use any grounds, places, buildings or facilities which may be offered, either temporarily or permanently, by individuals or corporations or other person whomsoever for playground or recreational purposes; it may, in the name of the City take and hold by purchase, devise, gift, bequest or otherwise such real and personal property as may be needful for carrying out the intents and purposes for which it is established; it shall recommend to the City Commissioners the institution of condemnation proceedings whenever, in its judgment, private property should be taken in the name of the City for the purpose of the Board of Public Recreation; it may, with the approval of the City Commissioners, sell and convey or lease lands whenever required by the recreational interests of the City and all proceeds from such sales or leases shall be deposited in the Treasury of the City to the credit of the Recreation Fund; it shall have the power for and in behalf of the City to receive donations, legacies, bequests for the improvement or maintenance of playgrounds, recreation centers or other recreational facilities, or the acquirement of new playgrounds, recreation centers, or other recreation places, and all moneys otherwise provided by the terms of such donations, legacies, bequests, be deposited in the Treasury of the City to the credit of the Recreation Fund; the same may be drawn therefrom and paid out only in the manner as is provided for the payment of moneys legally appropriated for the acquirement, support and improvement of such playgrounds, recreation centers and other recreation places; it shall have authority to organize and conduct plays, games, calisthenics, gymnastics, athletic sports, tournaments, meets, and leagues; dramatics, pageants, festivals and celebrations; community music, clubs, debating societies, public speaking, story telling, picnics, hikes, excursions, municipal camps, socials and any other form of activity that will employ the leisure time of the people in a constructive and wholesome manner.

Section 6. The Board of Public Recreation shall have power to appoint and employ superintendents, instructors and other officers and assistants and laborers; prescribe and fix their duties, authority, compensation and qualifications as to residence or otherwise; it shall have the exclusive management and disposal of all funds legally apportioned or received from any source for the support of playgrounds, recreation centers and other recreation facilities and activities; it shall have power to establish rules and regulations for the conduct of its officers and employees, and may require adequate bonds from any or all of them except laborers, for the faithful performance of their duties in such sums as may be fixed by it; such bonds shall be approved by the Mayor and the Auditor and filed in the office of the City Secretary; it shall have the power to formulate and adopt rules and regulations for the government of playgrounds, recreation centers and other recreation places and activities; not inconsistent with the ordinances of the City of Fort Worth or the Laws of the State of Texas or with this charter. The Board of Public Recreation will organize by electing one of its members President, one Vice-President, and one Secretary. The Board shall have the authority to elect a Secretary who is not a member of the Board. The officers shall hold office for one year and until their successors are elected. The Board shall hold regular meetings at least once in every two weeks and shall establish rules and regulations for its government and for the performance of its duties.

Section 7. The Board of Commissioners when levying the taxes for each fiscal year shall levy an ad valorem tax of not less than two cents nor more than five cents on each one hundred dollars of assessed value of all real and personal property in the City not exempt from taxation by the Constitution and the Laws of the State, for the use and the benefit of the Recreation Fund. Said tax when collected shall be deposited with the City Treasurer to the credit of the Recreation Fund and said sum, together with all sums appropriated by the City in the annual budget for recreational purposes, or received from other sources, shall be deposited and held by the City Treasurer in a separate account to the credit of the Recreation Fund, subject to the order and disbursement of the Board of Public Recreation for the purposes and in accordance with the authority herein specified and the same shall be paid out upon warrants issued by the Board of Public Recreation, signed by the President or Vice-President of said Board and countersigned by the City Auditor and the Secretary of the Board of Public Recreation.

Section 8. The Board of Commissioners of the City of Fort Worth shall have the authority to issue and sell bonds for the purchase and improvement of playgrounds, athletic fields, neigh-

borhood recreation parks; for the construction of swimming
pools, recreation center buildings and such other spaces and
facilities of a permanent nature deemed necessary for carrying
out the provisions of this Chapter of the City Charter, said bonds
to be issued and sold on such terms as may be prescribed by the
Board of Commissioners and in accordance with the limitations
prescribed by the Laws of the City and Constitution of the
State of Texas.

Section 9. The Secretary of the Board shall keep a full account of all property, money, receipts and expenditures and a
record of all proceedings of the Board. The votes of all its
members shall be recorded in the minutes with the ayes and noes.

Section 10. The Board of Commissioners may by ordinance
from time to time enlarge the authority and jurisdiction of the
Board of Public Recreation and confer upon it additional powers
not inconsistent with the law; and it is not intended by the fore-
going to fully define or limit the powers of said Board of Public
Recreation.[1]

What the future holds in the way of legislation for municipally conducted recreation is difficult to say. That the
movement of the past twelve years toward the creation of an
entirely new branch of the city government to deal with
recreation has grown out of the experience of a felt need
cannot be gainsaid. The park department in many cities had
not outlived the traditional concept of parks as beauty spots
rather than recreation centers. The school board was providing for the recreation of the school child. There had to
grow up an agency to provide for the younger-than-school-
age children, children out of school, and adults. Such an
agency has come in the form of a recreation department of
the city government.

The evils attendant upon the addition of a new branch to
the municipal governing body are obvious. Any extension

[1] Charter Provision, adopted 1922.

of the bureaucratic tendencies of our governments are questionable. Further than that, the already difficult problems of financing the local governments are enhanced. While the recreation department has won its way to a solid footing in many cities, it may be that in the future the park department will absorb this new agency and the powers and duties of that department will be enlarged. But even were that simplification to become a reality, there would still be a tendency to overlapping between the governmental body having to do with recreation and the school board. Either there must be cooperation between these two agencies in the employment of a recreation superintendent, as Nash suggests,[1] or the whole function of providing recreation must be intrusted to one body. And if the latter situation comes to pass, the school is certainly better prepared by location, equipment and past experience to assume the entire burden of municipal recreation.

[1] Nash, Jay B., *op. cit.*

CHAPTER III

OTHER FORMS OF MUNICIPALLY CONDUCTED RECREATION

THE range of activities embraced within a municipal recreation system are almost all-inclusive. While not always specifically enumerated they include parks, playgrounds, parkways and boulevards, athletic fields, bathing beaches and swimming pools, recreation centers, municipal auditoriums and stadia, plays, pageants and celebrations, gymnasiums, dance halls, summer camps and allied subjects. There are, however, several forms of municipally conducted recreation which are not included in this catalogue. Whether the municipal radio-broadcasting station belongs to this group is hard to determine. If it becomes a commercial agent such as the other radio-broadcasting stations, then it belongs with the billboard as a form of recreation! In any event, it can be excluded from this discussion on the ground that it is not a form of outdoor recreation. Likewise, the municipal airport belongs rather to the commercial than to the recreational field, although it is true that in a number of the state laws granting to cities powers concerning recreation, the power to establish municipal airports is included. It is conceivable that the municipal airport will come to be a recreational as well as a commercial center.

In addition to those forms of recreation over which the recreational department of the municipality has supervision, there are certain other types of municipally conducted recreation. And these types will be discussed here. They are municipal tourist camps, municipal music with primary emphasis on municipal band concerts, and town forests.

These topics may have the recreational features as of only secondary importance and yet they belong to a discussion of the provisions made by the city for the recreation of all the people. To the reader who lives in the eastern part of the United States, the first-named carries with it the notion of a cleared field with a hot-dog stand in one corner. Yet such is far from a true picture of the tourist camp as belonging to a study of public recreation. With respect to municipal music, such things as pageants, festivals and community sings belong to the functions of the department of recreation. The matter of the municipality employing a band to give free band concerts carries with it a whole body of legislation.

MUNICIPAL TOURIST CAMPS

Two considerations justify the inclusion of municipally owned and conducted tourist camps in a study of legislation for public outdoor recreation. The first of these is the fact that automobile tourist camping has become an important form of recreation. The automobile with all the equipment necessary for " camping out " has become a familiar sight on the highways of America. An interesting study awaits the sociologist of the future in making an investigation of the extent of this traffic, its influence on railway vacation travel, and its effect socially on health, public school attendance and socialization.

Now, if this camping meant merely the spending of a night in a camp and then going on, the tourist camp might very well be put in the same category as the hotel. But that kind of camp represents only one class, called by the League of Minnesota Municipalities,[1] the transit camp. But there is another type which this Bureau calls the terminal camp, " in

[1] League of Minnesota Municipalities, *Management and Control of Tourist Camps in Minnesota*, Univ. of Minn. Library, Minneapolis, Minn., 1926, 17 pp., p. 1.

which the tourist stays for a considerable length of time to obtain the recreational advantages of the surrounding territory ". In 1923, from figures compiled by the Denver Tourist's Bureau,[1] there were 650,000 tourists who visited Colorado and remained an average of seven days. How many of this number stayed at municipal tourist camps is not known; but the fact that 13 of 40 cities answering an inquiry in Colorado in 1923 reported [2] that it had been necessary to make regulations limiting the time that tourists might remain in camp to seven, ten, or fifteen days indicates that large numbers of the automobile tourists are making of the tourist camp a terminal camp. It also indicates that the tourist camp, especially in those places where no charge is made for the use of the camp, is giving rise to a new type of " hobo ", the automobile " hobo " who finds in the free tourist camp a cheap place to park his Ford and an inexpensive means of touring the country. This situation also gives rise to the need for a study of the new " hobo ".

A second consideration that justifies the inclusion of a study of the tourist camp here is the fact that it belongs in the same class as any other camp when it comes up to the standards such as those set by organizations like the Pacific Rocky Mountain Northwest Tourist Camp Conference.[3] These standards include not only the registration of persons and vehicles, sanitary provisions: toilets, lavatories, garbage cans, fuel, light, policing, pure water, but also a community house for recreational purposes, playgrounds, shower baths, cooking facilities, tables and benches, telephone service, and even a branch postoffice and a camp chaplain.

[1] *Proceedings of the Annual Convention of the State Association of Commercial Organizations of Colorado*, p. 18; Univ. Extension Division, Univ. of Colorado, Boulder, Colo., 1923, 43 pp.

[2] *Ibid.*, p. 34.

[3] *Ibid.*, pp. 21, 22.

Let it be understood then, that unless a tourist camp is something more than an open field, within or without the city limits, put at the disposal of the tourist by the municipal government at the instigation of the Rotary Club or some other boosters' organization, it cannot be regarded as a facility for outdoor recreation. The terminal camp at which the tourist stays for some time to enjoy the recreational advantages of the camp itself and of the surrounding country is the camp with which this discussion is concerned. And the camp must be operated by the municipality or the county as the governmental unit. In what ways do such camps offer recreational advantages? Bacon Park, West Palm Beach, Florida, is an interesting example. It is like a city built for recreational purposes. Its cost was in the neighborhood of $400,000. It has " its own water supply, sewerage system, garbage service, recreation hall, schools, stores, etc." [1] At Campe Grande, El Paso, Texas, in addition to all the usual accommodations appertaining to a camp, there are such facilities as a recreation hall, playground, reading rooms, and bus trips to points of scenic interest.

Some communities have found that the provision of a crude stage in the shelter house, or a platform out of doors encourages the campers to arrange impromptu entertainments or stunt shows among themselves. Many camps provide definite recreation or playground areas where such things as swings, sand boxes and wading pools are provided for the children, and horseshoe pitching, croquet or other games for the adults. In some communities the local park bands give regular concerts at the tourist camp for the entertainment of the visitors. [2]

---

[1] Florida State Board of Health, Bureau of Engineering, " Tourist Camps in Florida," *Bull. No. 3*, Jacksonville, 1926, 23 pp., p. 5.

[2] Wallis, Rolland S., " Tourist Camps," *Bulletin No. 56* of the Engineering Extension Dept. of Iowa State College, Ames, Iowa, July 8, 1925, 63 pp., pp. 32, 33.

Still other municipalities have provided dance halls, swimming pools, radio-receiving stations, basketball courts, seesaws, and bath houses in their tourist camps.

From these meager statements, it is apparent that the municipal tourist camp is an agency for promoting and adding to the facilities for recreation offered by the local community through its recreation system. To what extent, however, is it a public concern and not a private one conducted for commercial purposes? The American Automobile Association's Official Camping and Camp Site Manual for 1927 reports [1] there " are over three thousand approved motor camps in the United States and many more that may or may not be satisfactory ". Of this number 50 per cent may be said to be maintained by the city government. This figure is arrived at by comparison with the figures reached by the report of the Civic Development Department of the Chamber of Commerce of the United States of 1400 camps reporting in 1925.[2] Of this number, 701 were maintained by the city and the remainder by semi-public and private agencies. That it is a fair percentage of the total may be inferred from a study made of tourist camps in Minnesota in 1926, in which, of 175 camps reporting, 124 were owned by the city, or 71 per cent.[3] And of these 175, 134 offered either within or adjacent to the camp, one or all of these recreational features: drives, playgrounds, bathing beaches, boating and fishing.

The tourist-camp movement has arrived at considerable proportions. From questionnaires sent to 200 representative camps and from other sources, the Civic Development Department mentioned above came to the conclusion [4] in 1926

[1] P. 17.

[2] "Automobile Tourist Camps," 1926.

[3] *Op. cit.*, pp. 11-17.

[4] *Op. cit.*, p. 1.

that " There are in America today considerably over 2000 automobile tourist camps, representing an initial investment of about $10,000,000, costing over $4,000,000 to maintain and involving a tourist movement of 14,000,000 persons, who spent $20,000,000 in tourist camp communities." And in an earlier report (1922) this same department had said: " That a ten million dollar industry should grow up almost over night without attracting much attention is unusual even in this country of large-scale undertakings."

It is true that not much attention to the movement has been given by legislators, state or local, except in a regulatory way. The local government has set aside public land for the purpose of a camp and placed the administration in the hands of the park board or some other department or official of the government. In some instances the camp has been located on park property. Minnesota is the only state which has up to this time passed a law delegating power to municipalities to establish tourist camps. The text of this law follows:

That all cities, villages, towns and boroughs in the State of Minnesota are hereby authorized and empowered to establish and maintain public tourist camping grounds and the City Council or other legislative or governing body thereof is hereby empowered to acquire by lease, purchase, or by gift suitable lands located either within or without the corporate limits for use as public tourist camping grounds and to provide for the equipment, operation and maintenance of the same; provided, however, that the amount expended for the acquisition of any such public tourist camping grounds shall not exceed the sum of Six Thousand Dollars ($6000.00), and provided further that the amount that may be expended for the maintenance, improvement or operation of such tourist camping grounds shall not exceed in any one year a sum equal to the amount which may be raised by a one mill tax upon the taxable property of such municipality and in no event to exceed the sum of Five Thousand Dollars ($5000.00) per annum.[1]

[1] *Laws of Minnesota*, 1923, ch. 227.

Other states, notably Florida and Oregon, have passed laws providing that before any person, firm or corporation can establish a tourist camp, a permit must be obtained from the State Board of Health. These laws also give to the State Boards of Health or their agents general supervision regarding the camp and empower them to close the camps when they do not come up to the sanitary requirements of the boards. Thirty states [1] have through their Boards of Health enacted rules and regulations governing outdoor camps and to enforce them " special engineers or sanitary inspectors are employed during the summer months to supervise camp sanitation." These regulations are more or less uniform and cover such things as: keeping an attendant in charge, proper drainage of the camp, pure drinking water, toilet facilities, garbage and refuse disposal, posting of the rules and regulations, and provision for inspection and closing of the camp if it proves to be unsanitary. [2]

An ordinance carrying into effect the Florida law was passed by the City Council of Jacksonville, October 11, 1927. This ordinance, after defining the term tourist camp, provides that to establish a camp, any person, firm or corporation must obtain a permit from the City Council, which permit will be issued only after the City Health Department has been satisfied with regard to the location of the camp and the possible health problems involved. The City Commission is given authority to adopt rules and regulations governing the camp. In the City Health Department is vested the authority to close the camp if, on inspection, it is found to be unsanitary or unhealthful. A model ordinance creating a tourist camp, providing for the regulation thereof and establishing a fee

---

[1] *Bureau of Public Health Service, U. S. Treasury Dept.*, "Public Health Engineering Abstracts," June 25, 1927, p. 3.

[2] *Kansas Municipalities*, published by the League of Kansas Municipalities, June, 1926, pp. 9, 10.

for permits to camp therein has been prepared by the League of Kansas Municipalities as a guide to cities in that state which are considering the establishment of such camps. It is interesting to observe that this model ordinance provides that the camp is to constitute a part of the city park system. The full text of this ordinance is to be found in Appendix B.

Thus it is obvious that what state and local legislation there has been up to this time with regard to municipal tourist camps has been largely regulatory in nature and has been initiated by the boards of health. The problem has been one of safeguarding health and the question of whether or not the municipality has the power to establish such camps has been a secondary consideration. If the municipality increasingly adds this function to its operations, additional state legislation similar to that in Minnesota will be necessary. This was forcefully demonstrated by the Kansas City, Mo. Court of Appeals when the court decided [1] that the city had no authority to conduct tourist camps and could not be held liable for nuisance since their operation was *ultra vires*. The court said further that the operation of tourist camps does not fall within statutory or charter authority to own and operate public parks.

Precisely the same problem arises in connection with the municipal vacation camp for children. In 184 cities in 1926, such camps were being conducted by the city government under the supervision of the park board, the recreation department or some other department of the government. The city of Oakland, California, which conducted such summer camps under its recreation program found it necessary several years ago to change its charter to allow the recreation department to conduct such activities outside the city. Because of the difficulty which has been met here and other places, the

---

[1] Kennedy *v*. City of Nevada (281 S. W. 56).

state laws and the local ordinances or charter provisions should embrace within their powers, the power to have the municipal recreation system extend beyond the usual limits of the municipality.

MUNICIPAL MUSIC

If music were of only educational importance, it would not belong to this study.   But it is also a form of recreation. When Kenneth S. Clark of the National Bureau for the Advancement of Music made a report to the National Recreation Congress meeting in Atlantic City, October 18, 1924, of the survey which he was making of municipal music in America, that congress saw fit to include in its promotive activities the problem of municipal music.   To that end the congress adopted a resolution, part of which reads as follows:

Resolved, that it is the opinion of this Recreation Congress that the various municipal governments should, in the expansion of their recreation programs, give increasing attention to the question of the municipal appropriation which shall aid in meeting the city's growing needs in the providing of such activities as open-air band concerts, a community orchestra, municipal organ recitals, a civic auditorium, community singing, civic opera, or other musical advantages which may be needed to enrich the city's community life, and be it further

Resolved, that the Playground and Recreation Association of America be requested to appoint a committee to cooperate during the coming year with the efforts to bring about more encouragement of music by the municipal governments of our country.[1]

The first of these activities mentioned in these resolutions, namely, the open-air band concerts has been the chief concern, up to this time, of the municipal music program in this country.   Just as the legislation of the states on municipal

[1] Clark, Kenneth S., *Municipal Aid to Music in America*, National Bureau for the Advancement of Music, New York, 1925, 297 pp., p. 16.

recreation was aimed primarily at giving power to the local units to spend public money for that purpose, so the main intent of state legislation covering municipal music has been the authorization of tax levies by cities for music. The method of considering these laws will be to embody here, as in the previous analyses, examples of state acts representing varieties of provisions, and then a summary digest of the provisions of all the state laws on this specific subject will be presented in Appendix C.

Alabama — The counties, cities, and towns in the state of Alabama may appropriate moneys out of their general funds for the maintenance and support of municipal bands and other musical organizations for public entertainment.[1]

Maine — Cities and towns may raise money for the maintenance or employment of a band of music for municipal purposes and public celebrations. The provisions of this act shall not be in force in any city or town unless approved by a majority vote of the qualified voters of such city or town at an annual election.[2]

Illinois — Sec. 1. Any incorporated city, village or town having a population of less than five hundred thousand may, when authorized as hereinafter provided, levy each year a tax not exceeding one (1) mill on the dollar for the maintenance or employment of a municipal band for musical purposes.

Sec. 2. Such authority shall be initiated by a petition signed by five per cent (5%) of the legal voters of the incorporated city, village or town as shown by the last regular municipal election. Said petition shall be filed with the clerk of the city, village or town, and shall request that the following question be submitted to the voters, to wit: " Shall a tax not exceeding . . . mills be levied each year on all taxable property in the . . . of . . . for the purpose of providing a fund for the maintenance or employment of a municipal band for musical purposes? "

[1] Ch. 43, art. 25, sec. 2056, code 1923.
[2] *Laws of Maine*, 1927, ch. 24.

Sec. 3. When such petition is filed, the council must cause the question to be submitted to the voters at the next general municipal election. (Form of ballot and method of voting.)

Sec. 4. The levy shall be authorized if the majority of the votes cast at the election are in favor of said proposition, and the council shall then levy a tax sufficient to maintain or employ such band not exceeding one (1) mill on the assessed valuation of the property in such municipality, and not exceeding the amount stated in the petition: Provided, that said annual tax shall not be included in the aggregate amount of taxes as limited by section 1 of Article VIII of " An Act for the incorporation of cities and villages ", approved April, 10, 1872, as amended, and the county clerk in reducing tax levies under the provisions of section 2 of " An Act concerning levy and extension of taxes " approved May 9, 1901, as amended, shall not include said tax in the limitation of one per cent of the assessed valuation upon which taxes are required to be extended.

Sec. 5. A petition, signed by five per cent (5%) of the legal voters of the incorporated city, village or town as shown by the last regular municipal election may at any time be filed with the council requesting that the following question be submitted to the voters, to wit, " Shall the power to levy a tax for the purpose of providing a fund for the maintenance or employment of a municipal band for musical purposes be cancelled? " The council must submit this question at the next general municipal election, and if the majority of the votes cast be in favor of said cancellation, no further levy for such purpose shall be made.

Sec. 6. All funds derived from the said levy shall be expended as provided in section 1 of this Act.[1]

From these illustrations and the summary digest of specific state legislation to be found in Appendix C, it is not to be assumed that within the remaining states, municipalities cannot appropriate money to provide musical entertainment for the people. Either the grants of power made to municipal

[1] *Laws of Ill.*, 1925, p. 204; Am. 1927, *Laws*, 1927, pp. 258-9.

corporations by the state concerning the making of appropriations, or a liberal interpretation of charters in states having constitutional home-rule may be and have been construed to cover appropriations made for music. As early as
1886, long before Massachusetts had any specific law author-
izing cities and town to appropriate funds for municipal
music, the Supreme Court in the case of Hubbard *v.* City of
Taunton [1] upheld the right of the city to expend money for
band concerts under the general grant of powers given to
towns and cities to appropriate not over one fiftieth of one
per cent of the property valuation for armories, celebrations
of holidays, and for other public purposes. The court placed
this under " other public purposes."

From the above mentioned work by Mr. Clark,[2] it is to be
noted that in 762 cities and towns answering his questionnaire, the annual governmental expenditure for music, not
including that expended for public school music, was approximately $1,250,000. Of this expenditure, about 75 per cent
is spent on band concerts. The remaining 25 per cent is
scattered among orchestras, city organists, community
observance of National Music Week, etc. While not significant in the amount of money expended by the government,
since symphony orchestras have in the past been largely supported by private subscription and endowment, it is significant that " Atlanta, Pittsburgh, Portland, Me., Memphis,
Tenn., Baltimore, Md., and Denver, Colo., are spending
public funds for such objects as public organists, municipal
bands and orchestras, directors of music, etc." [3]

In the nature of the case, the only legislative action on the
part of the municipality under these state laws is to make an

---

[1] 140 Mass. 467.

[2] *Op. cit.,* p. 63.

[3] *Civic Development Department of the U. S. Chamber of Commerce,*
" The Movement for Symphony Orchestras in American Cities," 1925.

appropriation for music or to levy a tax or to entertain a petition from a certain per cent of the qualified voters calling for a referendum on the question.   There are no ordinances to be considered, therefore, in connection with this subject. The only city in the country which has a department of music as a part of the city government is Baltimore, Maryland, and consequently its experience deserves a brief mention.   This department was created by action of the Board of Estimates at a special meeting held May 10, 1918.   The following extract is from the minutes of that meeting:

Mr. Frederick R. Huber was appointed Director of Music for Baltimore City. His duties will be to attend to not only the Baltimore Symphony Orchestra, which he has been attending to in the past, but also to the Municipal Band. He will have entire control of time, places, and programs for the concerts. His salary will be $500.00 for the season beginning May 1, 1918.[1]

The unique feature of Baltimore's system is that this Director of Music heads a municipal department of music responsible only to the Mayor and Council.   No private subscriptions are accepted for any of the musical activities, the appropriation for such activities being made from the tax budget. The city now has a budget especially for music which calls for an annual expenditure of approximately $100,000. Part of this amount is derived from a special tax on transit facilities.   The city supports not only a park symphony orchestra, but a municipal band in addition to the Baltimore Symphony Orchestra. The latter orchestra is the only organization of its kind in the country supported by the taxpayers of a city.

[1] *Extract from Minutes of Special Meeting of Board of Estimates,* James Thrift, Sec'y., dated May 10, 1918.

TOWN FORESTS

A subject which deserves mention in any summary of legislation for outdoor recreation is that of town forests. Eleven states have passed laws empowering municipalities to acquire land for town forests and to appoint a town forester. To be sure, the primary purpose in the enactment of such laws and the establishment of such forests is an economic one, namely, that of providing a town with a source of income and a timber supply, in addition to the opportunity it offers for employing labor. And the economic purpose is the one which has had the most attention up to this time. But with the growth of the movement, the secondary purposes, those of providing educational advantages to school children and recreational facilities for the community will receive increasing attention. That these purposes were in the minds of the legislators in passing these laws is evidenced from the following extracts from the Massachusetts law and the Maine law of 1927:

Massachusetts: " Any city or town owning a public domain may lease any building thereon, and it may erect thereon any building for public instruction and recreation." [1]

Maine: " Any city or town owning such forest area may lease any building thereon, and may erect thereon any building for public instruction and recreation." [2]

In the state of Massachusetts, 77 of the 356 municipalities have established such forests with an acreage of 9,589 acres. For every town that will create a forest of 100 acres or more, the Massachusetts Forestry Association agrees to plant free of charge 5000 trees or approximately five acres. In Vermont, 33 out of about 300 communities have established such areas, totaling 6,575 acres. The recreational advant-

---

[1] *General Laws of Mass.*, 1921, ch. 45, sec. 22.

[2] *Laws of Maine*, 1927, ch. 33, sec. 4.

age which the forests in these and other states offer consist in camping areas, picnic grounds, game refuges and hunting and fishing grounds.

BIBLIOGRAPHY

American City Bureau, Research Division—Automobile Camping Grounds, *Report No. 510*, New York, July, 1921.

American Tree Association, *Forestry Primer*, Washington, D. C., 1926.

"Baltimore Leads Country in Municipal Music," *Baltimore Municipal Journal*, Jan. 24, 1927.

Florida State Board of Health, monthly bulletin, Sept., 1927, Jacksonville, *State Tourist Camp Law*, pp. 118-120.

Massachusetts Forestry Association, "Town Forests, the Massachusetts Plan," *Bull. 137*, Boston, Jan., 1924, 8 pp.

National Conference on State Parks, *State Recreation* for Feb., 1927.

Playground and Recreation Association of America, *Community Music*.

Proceedings of the State Association of Commercial Organizations of Colorado, Fourth Annual Convention, University Extension Division, Univ. of Colorado, Boulder, 1925, 58 pp.

Straus, Henrietta, "A Municipal Exploit in Music," *Nation*, May 7, 1924.

Tisdale, E. S., "Tourist Camps," *Circular 274*, Agricultural Extension Division, College of Agriculture, West Virginia University, Morgantown, June 1924, 11 pp.

Vermont Forest Association, "Municipal Forests and Forestry in Vermont," *Bull. 2*, Northfield, Vt., Jan., 1927.

CHAPTER IV

Liabilities of Cities When Conducting Public Outdoor Recreation

The subjects considered in the previous chapters, namely, tourist camps, municipal music and town forests together with the activities over which the recreation department of the local government has supervision, cover the main features of a city's outdoor recreation program. The movement to create such a recreation department has raised some very interesting problems. There are not only questions of organization, powers, and means of financing; there is also the issue of liability. Can a municipal corporation be held liable in a damage suit to recover for injuries suffered on public recreation areas? The number of cases arising may be comparatively insignificant, but the variety of court opinions rendered on the subject makes up for the decreasing proportion of cases. From the standpoint of a city executive, it is rather important for him to know the precedent in his state with regard to court decisions on this point. Otherwise he might find public opinion turning decidedly against public recreation if the taxpayers are required to pay a $10,000 damage arising from a tort action. It is not sufficient to dismiss the problem by saying that the majority of the courts have declared that this is a function analogous to the health and fire departments and hence the city is not liable. There is too wide a diversity in such court opinions.

Can a municipal corporation be held liable for injuries suffered on recreation areas due either to the negligence of the city itself or its employees? From the preceding discussion with regard to the relation between the local and the state governments it was apparent that the traditional view of this relationship is that the local government is a creation of the state government deriving its powers from the latter and subject to its sovereign will. Two distinct functions the municipality may be said to discharge: (1) those powers granted to it either expressly or implied in its creation by the state government; (2) those powers "essential to the accomplishment of the declared objects and purposes of the corporation ".[1] Now the state when it is exercising its public functions cannot be held liable for torts. This is what is known as the governmental function and arises from the traditional concept that "the king can do no wrong". By analogy, therefore, the municipal government, when it is engaged in performing functions similar to those performed by the state and is acting as the agent of the state, is acting in a governmental capacity and is not liable for torts. On the other hand the local unit engages in functions which belong to "the economic life of its citizens . . . . which were formerly conducted by individuals or private corporations, often enterprises not essential to good government but which are more in the nature of conveniences." [2] Such functions are termed private or proprietary.

The distinction between these two types of functions gives rise to much of the confusion resulting from the decisions which are to be considered in this chapter. Just what activities of the municipal government are generally regarded as governmental and which private or proprietary has been well expressed by the Court in the case of City of Trenton *v.* State of New Jersey: [3]

[1] Dillon, J. F., *op. cit.*
[2] Warden *v.* City of Grafton, 128 S. E. 375 (1925).
[3] 262 U. S. 182.

It has been held that municipalities are not liable for such acts and omissions in the exercise of the police power, or in the performance of such municipal faculties as the erection and maintenance of a city hall and court house, the protection of the city's inhabitants against disease and unsanitary conditions, the care of the sick, the operation of fire departments, the inspection of steam boilers, the promotion of education and the administration of public charities. On the other hand they have been held liable when such acts or omissions occur in the exercise of the power to build and maintain bridges, streets and highways, and waterworks, construct sewers, collect refuse and care for the dump where it is deposited. Recovery is denied where the act or omission occurs in the exercise of what are deemed to be governmental powers, and is permitted if it occurs in a proprietary capacity. The basis of the distinction is difficult to state, and there is no established rule for the determination of which belongs to the one or the other class. It originated with the courts.

It is to be expected then that since this distinction between governmental and proprietary functions is difficult to state and since it originated with the courts, there will be considerable diversity of opinion on the part of the courts as to whether public recreation is a governmental or a proprietary function. And that is precisely the case. The American Law Review in a discussion of these cases, says,[1] " A majority of the cases, taking into consideration that parks are established with the view and purpose of furnishing to the people at large a place for free recreation to promote the health and general welfare of the public, support the view that a municipality, in maintaining a public park, is engaged in a governmental activity,—discharging a public duty,— and is therefore not liable for injuries caused through negligent conditions therein ". While it is true that in the states

[1] 29 A. L. R. 863 (1924).

where a decision has been rendered, the majority of the opinions declare the function to be a governmental one, the majority is not an imposing one as will appear from the following analysis.

On several points in these cases the courts are rather well agreed: (1) negligence must be shown; (2) the fact that incidental revenue might be derived from the conduct of recreation does not alter the character of the function. On the question of the liability of the city for damages sustained, however, there is no such general agreement. In Norberg *v.* Hagna et al,[1] the plaintiff sued the officers of the city of Watertown, South Dakota, for injuries sustained while diving off a diving board in a lake within a park owned and maintained by the city. The court said:

A municipal corporation is liable for negligence in permitting obstructions or defects in its streets or sidewalks. . . . Why then should it not be liable for the negligence in question? We confess our inability to perceive any valid reason why a distinction should be made between streets and public parks in the matter of liability for negligence. They are both open to general public travel and use, without reference to the residence of the traveler.

In another case, Caughlan *v.* Omaha,[2] in which the facts were very similar except that the diver suffered death, the court held that " The rule generally adopted is that, in the absence of statute, a city, in maintaining a public park or a municipal beach is not pecuniarily liable for the negligence of city officers while exercising functions relating to this feature of municipal government." Two judges dissented from this opinion on the ground that the city in operating parks is acting independently and in its own interests, and that the function

[1] 195 N. W. 438 (1923).
[2] 103 Neb. 726 (1919).

was no more governmental than that of laying out, constructing and caring for its streets.

Two cases decided by two State Supreme Courts as recently as April 1927, indicate the opposed views of the courts. In Hannon *v.* Waterbury,[1] the Supreme Court of Connecticut held that the municipality was immune from liability to tort action resulting from negligence in the conduct of a public park. But in Longmount *v.* Swearington,[2] the Supreme Court of Colorado held that the city was liable for negligence in failing to provide a life guard at a municipal swimming pool.

The question raised by the South Dakota court and the dissenting opinion of the Nebraska judges as to the similarity between the function of caring for the streets and the conduct of public recreation has also been raised by other jurisdictions. For instance, the Utah court in Alder *v.* Salt Lake City[3] decided that the city was not liable for injuries sustained by a child in the collapse of a stand erected in connection with a pageant offered under the supervision of the recreation department. While it is true, the court said, that municipalities are liable for negligence in the maintenance and care of public streets, such exception is " founded upon public policy and expediency, and is recognized in the state by legislative act. . . . If the exception is to be extended to parks and playgrounds, the legislature and not the courts should determine the question." The Michigan court in Heino *v.* City of Grand Rapids[4] refused damages to the father of a child drowned in a public swimming pool and bathing pool. The ground for the decision was that the function was being exercised without private gain to the

[1] 136 Atl. 876 (1927).

[2] 254 Pac. 1000 (1927).

[3] 64 Utah 568 (1924).

[4] 202 Mich. 363 (1918).

corporation and was therefore a governmental function. Such a decision the court said was perfectly in accord with the rulings of the Michigan court that damages could not be recovered from a city due to negligence in the construction and maintenance of streets.

On the question of incidental revenue, on which it was said above that the courts were rather well agreed, it is interesting to note that the Michigan court in Foss v. City of Lansing [1] said that incidental revenue derived from the conduct of public recreation did change the character of the case sufficient to give grounds for action. In such cases, the court held that the municipality is liable the same as private corporations would be. However, when the question has been raised, the courts have for the most part declared that incidental revenue does not alter the nature of the case.[2] The city is not conducting the facility for the sake of profit as a commercial agent would do.

Some jurisdictions have interpreted the function of conducting recreation as a proprietary one and have based their decisions as to liability on no other consideration. In Warden v. City of Crafton,[3] the court awarded damages to the plaintiff for injuries sustained to a finger due to a ring catching on a protruding bolt of a slide. In substance the court held that where the municipality was exercising functions " formerly conducted by individuals or private corporations, often enterprises not essential to good government, but which are more in the nature of conveniences and places of amusement and recreation," it was operating in a proprietary capacity. In Bloom v. City of Newark,[4] the Ohio court held that the power granted to cities by the state to lay out and

[1] 212 N. W. 952 (1927).

[2] Blair v. Granger, 24 R. I. 17; Caughlan v. Omaha, 103 Nebraska 726.

[3] 128 S. E. 375 (1925).

[4] 3 Ohio N. P. N. S. 480 (1905).

maintain parks was permissive only, to be exercised or not as the city saw fit. The fact that the city chose to exercise the power, when the state had no interest in the power so exercised made the city liable. And in a similar vein, the Indiana court reasoned in Kokomo *v.* Loy,[1] that " where a power is given and a duty imposed, a corresponding liability arises for the proper exercise thereof." But, on the contrary, the Supreme Court of Tennessee in Mayor and City Council of Nashville *v.* Burns [2] refused damages to a child injured by a swing in a public park on the ground that the function was a governmental one.[3]

Following the method adopted in the consideration of the legislative enactments, it might be well to summarize and place in juxtaposition these judicial decisions in order to see the divergence of opinion with regard to this question. The cases are from thirty jurisdictions and they group themselves into two main divisions; the first, those cases in which the court made the municipality non-liable and the second those in which the court declared the local government to be liable. In the latter group, those cases will be presented first in which the court declared the function to be a proprietary one and then those cases in which nothing was said about the nature of the function.

---

[1] 185 Ind. 18 (1916).

[2] 131 Tenn. 281 (1914).

[3] See also Blair *v.* Granger, 24 Rhode Island 17 (1902) ; Board of Park Commissioners *v.* Prinz, 127 Ky. 460 (1907) ; Russell *v.* City of Tacoma, 8 Wash. 156 (1894) ; Bernstein *v.* City of Milwaukee, 158 Wis. 576 (1914).

I. Non-Liability

Case	Grounds for Decision
Nashville *v.* Burns (131 Tenn. 281), 1914	Governmental function
Heino *v.* Grand Rapids (202 Mich. 363), 1918	Governmental function — pool not an attractive nuisance
Blair *v.* Granger (24 R. I. 17), 1902	Governmental function—incidental revenue does not make city liable
Board of Park Com. *v.* Prinz (127 Ky. 460), 1907	Governmental function
Emmons *v.* Virginia *et al.* (152 Minn. 295), 1922	Governmental function even though voluntarily undertaken
Harper *v.* Topeka (92 Kan. 11) 1914	Governmental function — pond not an attractive nuisance
Caughlan *v.* Omaha (103 Neb. 726), 1919	Governmental function — incidental revenue does not alter
Alder *v.* Salt Lake City (64 Utah 568), 1924	Governmental function even though voluntarily undertaken
Nelson *v.* Tacoma (104 Wash. 219), 1918	Governmental function
Bernstein *v.* Milwaukee (158 Wis. 576), 1914	Governmental function but if this had been public nuisance city would be liable
Warrenton *v.* Smith (149 Ga. 567), 1919	Governmental function
Kellar *v.* Los Angeles (179 Calif. 605), 1919	Governmental function
Hannon *v.* Waterbury (136 Atl. 876), 1927	Governmental function
Hensley *v.* Gowrie (212 N. W. 714), 1927	Governmental function — care of parks not analogous to care of streets
Bisbing *v.* Asbury Park (80 N. J. L. 416), 1910	Governmental function
Bolster *v.* Lawrence (225 Mass. 387), 1917	Governmental function
Vanderford *v.* Houston (286 S. W. 568), 1926	Governmental function

II. Liability

Case	Grounds for Decision
Warden *v.* Grafton (128 S. E. 375), 1925	Proprietary function
Kokomo *v.* Loy (185 Ind. 18), 1916	Proprietary function
Bloom *v.* City of Newark (3 Ohio N.P.N.S. 480), 1905	Proprietary function — ci voluntarily undertak function
Ramirez *v.* Cheyenne (241 Pac. Rep. 710), 1925	Proprietary function
Norberg *v.* Hagna (195 N. W. 438), 1923	Proprietary function—an logous to streets
Haithcock *v.* Columbia (115 S. C. 29), 1920	Function analogous to kee. ing streets in repair
Barthold *v.* Philadelphia (154 Penn 109), 1893	Maintenance of nuisance on public grounds
Capp *v.* St. Louis (251 Mo. 345), 1913	Parks must be kept in rea- sonably safe condition
Longmount *v.* Swearingen (254 Pac. 1000), 1927	City guilty of negligence
Silverman *v.* New York (114 N. Y. Supp. 59), 1909	City bound to exercise or dinary care
Boise Development Co. *v.* Boise (30 Idaho 675), 1917	Proprietary function
Anadarko *v.* Swain (42 Okla. 741), 1914	City owed to children visit- ing parks reasonable car to avoid injuring them
Pennell *v.* Wilmington (7 Pennewill Del. 229), 1906	Board of Park Commis- sioners similar to City': Street and Sewer De- partment

There is no single clear-cut issue over which the courts have divided on this question of liability. The nearest approach to an issue is whether or not the function is a governmental one or a proprietary one. But not all of the decisions quoted have even raised the question of the nature of t' function. In several instances the courts have merely sa that it is the duty of the municipality to see to it that i parks, playgrounds, and recreation areas are kept in a reaso ably safe condition. Is the question of negligence then t' issue? No, it is not, because in many of the decisions making the local government non-liable the question of negligence does not enter since even if negligence could be shown, the function is governmental and the municipality therefore not liable. Might the issue be one of maintaining an " attractive nuisance " ? In some instances,[1] the courts have held that even though the nature of the function be governmental, the city may be held liable if it can be shown that there has been maintained an " attractive nuisance ".

While a majority of the thirty jurisdictions here analyzed regard the conduct of recreation a governmental function and have declared the cities non-liable, it is by no means uniformly recognized. At least twelve states through their courts have said the " municipal corporations are under a duty of exercising reasonable care in the maintenance of parks and other public enterprises of like character ".[2]

It may be objected that this discussion of the liability of the municipality when conducting a recreation program is not of sufficient importance to be included in this study. Figures are not available as to the number of accidents occurring on recreation spaces other than the results of a questionnaire sent out a few years ago to park and recreation authorities in the principal cities of the United States and Canada. O. W. Douglas in reporting the results of this study says:[3] " reports received show a total attendance of over 35,000,000 for 1924 from which we glean the following: Total number of accidents reported, 334, or less than 1 to 100,000 in attendance ". But while the number of accidents is small and according to the Playground and Recreation Association of America, with the improvements in the

[1] 108 Wis. 359; 101 Tenn. 342; 154 Mass. 511.

[2] *Op. cit.* Warden *v.* Grafton.

[3] Douglas, O. W., " Park and Playground Accidents," *Parks and Recreation*, vol. ix, Nov.-Dec., 1925, p. 214.

character of playground apparatus, this number is becoming even smaller, it is quite conceivable that if a city were held for several damage suits in large amounts in connection with such accidents it might have considerable influence on the attitude of public opinion toward recreation in that community.

It would seem to be very important, at least, for the recreation executive in a locality to know what the attitude of the courts in his state was toward this problem of liability. Such information is necessary if the recreation program is to be protected by liability insurance. In New York State, for example, where the courts have been holding the municipality liable, a study was made in 1925 by the New York State Bureau of Municipal Information to determine whether municipalities were carrying such liability insurance. The following are extracts from that report:[1]

Batavia reports that the city did not carry last year but this year took liability in 20/20 amounts. Their playgrounds are conducted by a separate organization and not under city management, but they have arranged it so that the city liability covers them.

In Dunkirk, the Board of Education carries public liability insurance covering injuries to children using playgrounds, as well as other equipment of the school system. This policy also covers any injuries that may be sustained by the general public. The insurance is limited to a payment of $10,000 to any one individual and to a payment of $50,000 as the result of any one accident.

In the following cities the matter of carrying such insurance is under consideration: Oswego, Little Falls, Newburgh, Canandaigua.

Reasonable uniformity has been reached by court decisions

[1] New York State Bureau of Municipal Information, *Liability Insurance Covering Users of Playgrounds, Report No. 2080*, Sept. 28, 1925.

and state statutes concerning the liability of municipalities for accidents arising from the maintenance of streets and highways.   The function is usually considered a proprietary one and the courts have consistently held and the state legislatures have enacted statutes making the city liable.   But no such uniformity seems to be possible on the question of accidents on recreation areas.   It would seem then that the controversy should be settled in the legislature.   There is a definite need for legislative enactment within the various states setting forth the immunity or the liability of a municipality when conducting a program of recreation.   Such a law declaring the municipality immune has been enacted by South Dakota.[1]   This is the only state legislation on the subject.

No action shall lie against the board or against the city or the governing body of the city to recover for injuries sustained by any person through the negligence of the officers or employees of the board while engaged in the improvement, maintenance or operation of land owned or operated as a park or for park purposes, provided, however that nothing herein contained shall operate to prevent any employee of the board or of the city from maintaining an action to recover damages for injuries received in the course of his employment.

BIBLIOGRAPHY

American Law Review, vol. 60, pp. 615-619; vol. 59, pp. 565-567.

"A Supreme Court Discusses Municipal Liability," *American City*, Oct., 1926, pp. 485-488.

Nash, Jay B., *Organization and Administration of Playgrounds and Recreation*, A. S. Barnes and Co., New York, 1927, 547 pp., ch. vi.

" Parks and Playgrounds—Liability for Negligence," *National Municipal Review*, July, 1927, p. 476.

Playground and Recreation Association of America, *Liability for Playground Accidents*, compiled from statements on the subject from various sources, July, 1926, 6 pp. typewritten.

[1] Ch. 237, Acts of 1925, amending sec. 6508, *Revised Code of South Dakota*, 1919.

CHAPTER V

STATE AND FEDERAL PROVISIONS FOR PUBLIC OUTDOOR RECREATION

NOTHING beyond suggestion has as yet come of the movement for a nation plan whereby the whole country may be planned in advance to provide a coordinated system of highways and recreational areas to care for the future needs of the people. Suffice it to say that the city, county, state and federal provisions for recreation have been made largely in an independent manner. In some instances, viz., the New York Council on State Parks, an effort has been made to visualize a state plan making effective coordination between the county units and the state. And there has been some attempt, such as that shown by the cooperation of the Westchester County Commission and the authorities of New York City with regard to the Bronx Parkway, to have county and city units work together. In Cuyahoga County, Ohio, the first steps have been taken to bring about such coordination between the county and the local units. " For, voluntarily, the municipal engineers, the members of planning commissions, and the mayors of most of these fifty villages and four cities have banded themselves under the name of ' The Cuyahoga Planning Congress ' and have set about to create one great and ambitious plan for the entire territory embraced within the county." [1]

[1] Metzenbaum, James, " Planning the Main Thoroughfares and Open Spaces for an Entire Region," *American City*, New York, November, 1927, p. 581.

Likewise between the state and the local units there has been some cooperation in this matter of providing properly located recreation areas. By the provisions of a New York Law passed in 1923, the state engineer is given power to convey to a city, town or county, for the consideration of one dollar, any parcel or parcels of land owned by the State and useful for local park, recreation, playground and reforestration purposes. Upon such transfer to the local authorities, such parcels must be properly improved and maintained for such purposes.[1] Also, between states there has been an attempt to look beyond mere state boundaries in creating regional parks. Examples of such parks are the Palisades Inter-State Park of New York and New Jersey, the Taconic Tri-State Park operated by three states, Massachusetts, Connecticut and New York, and the combination between Minnesota and Wisconsin in the Taylor's Falls State Park and the St. Croix Falls State Park. Such regional parks are managed and controlled by a joint commission appointed from the states involved.

But while these and other efforts at coordination and cooperation have proved to be very successful, the fact remains that the local, county, state and federal agencies have, up to this time, largely operated independently and without either the vision or the means at hand to plan a nation-wide coordination of the facilities for recreation. Local recreation leaders find it difficult to get the cooperation necessary even between different branches of the municipal government. How much more difficult, therefore, will it be to get the proper coordination between local and county, county and state, and state and federal agencies! But while the time may be far distant, the examples of cooperation between governmental agencies which have been cited above merely

---

[1] " State Land for Playgrounds," *The Playground*, New York, vol. xvii, 1923, p. 451.

point the way to what will be an absolute necessity in the future, namely, the working together of the planning agencies of all the governmental divisions to achieve a nation-wide coordination of highways, recreational areas, and the other elements involved in planning.

The movement to establish state parks is a phenomenon of the last fifty years. The first state park in the United States, exclusive of the " Great Ponds " of Massachusetts, was what is now the Yosemite National Park, given by the federal government to California by act of Congress in 1863, but not taken over completely by the state until 1875. The Niagara State Reservation of New York in 1885; Mackinac Island, accepted by Michigan from the United States government in the same year; and the Birch Coulie Park, set aside by Minnesota in 1889, were among the first state parks in this country. Despite these beginnings, however, little was done before the opening of the present century. The intensive movement for state parks belongs to the last twelve years or the period covered by this study. In 1921, only twenty states had taken steps toward the establishment of state parks; in 1927 forty-three of the forty-eight states had either acquired areas for parks or had taken the necessary steps to their acquisition. " There are now more than 500 state parks and forests throughout the nation with a total area of over four million acres, and within easy access of three-quarters of the population ".[1]

In any discussion of state parks in connection with their recreational advantages, state forests are usually included, together with state-park monuments and state-park memorials. The latter two, which are areas set aside to commemorate some person or event of historic importance are not of sufficient acreage to affect the general conclusions re-

[1] Ward, Beatrice M., " Developing State Parks," 4 pp., reprinted from the December, 1927 issue of the *National Republic*.

garding recreational areas. What then is a state park? As defined by Col. Richard Lieber, Director of the Conservation Commission of Indiana,[1] it includes the following:

A state park must have either scenic or historical value, or both. The state park is an area whose primary purpose is the preservation of a portion of the soil of the commonwealth of natural beauty and significance in unspoiled primitiveness. Whatever else it may offer the citizen in the physical pleasures of outings, camping, hiking, fishing, nature study and recreation, its primary mission is this: the keeping intact and "unimproved" for all generations to come a part of Nature's original domain.

Such a definition of a state park places the preservation of natural scenic beauty as the primary purpose and recreational utility as the secondary consideration. While such is undoubtedly the ideal toward which the agencies in this field are working, actually, Barrington Moore is probably correct when he says:[2] "The purpose of parks is to preserve scenery, natural and historic objects, and plants and wild life, for recreation, for science and for education, both for this and for future generations. Although the primary incentive for creating State parks has been recreation, the use of parks in science and education is growing rapidly." The reason for this conclusion is to be found in seeking for an explanation of the fact that the intensive movement for state parks is a recent phenomenon. In the first twenty-five years of state-park history, twelve states had entered the field; in the last twenty-five years, thirty-one additional states have come in. There are three possible answers to the question of how to account for this sudden growth of interest in state parks.

[1] Moore, Barrington, *A State Park every Hundred Miles*, Bulletin, National Conference on State Parks, Washington, D. C., 9 pp., p. 4.

[2] *Ibid.*, p. 7.

(1) The promotive work of the National Conference on State Parks. This conference was organized in 1921 at the suggestion of the Hon. Stephen T. Mather, Director of the National Park Service. Many demands had come to the federal park service for the creation of national parks which the Department of the Interior could not meet or would not meet because of the failures of the areas to come up to the qualifications of a national park. But Director Mather felt they were of sufficient importance to be taken care of and that the state should be the agency to provide for them. Since the organization of the National Conference the movement has advanced rapidly. It is interesting to note that in the objects of the Conference, as formulated by it, recreation occupies first place: [1]

To urge upon our governments, local, county, state and national, the acquisition of land and water areas suitable for recreation and preservation of wild life, as a form of the conservation of our natural resources, until eventually there shall be public parks, forests, and preserves within easy access of all the people of our nation, and also to encourage the interest of non-governmental agencies, and individuals in acquiring, maintaining and dedicating for public use similar areas; and as a means of cementing all park interests into a harmonious whole, to provide for a conference and exchange of ideas by an annual meeting of such interests and the formation of facilities for the exchange of information and ideas between conferences.

(2) The conservation movement set in motion by President Roosevelt at the now famous Conference of Governors at the White House in 1907. No one doubts the significance of this conference in promoting the movement for conservation. However, the movement has been largely in that field with recreation only a secondary consideration.

[1] *State Recreation*, monthly bulletin issued by National Conference on State Parks, Washington, D. C.

(3) The public demand for recreation areas brought about by increase of travel, and especially automobile travel. Mr. Raymond T. Torrey[1] has well emphasized this point, showing that along with the demand for highways, there came an increasing demand for places to see, sites on which to camp, and areas set aside for rest and recreation. An interesting example of this association between highways and parks is to be found in the state of Oregon, where the state highway department is in charge of the administration of state parks.

That the first and last of these factors have been largely responsible for the impetus given to the state-park program of the past twelve years, there can be no question. And that the last named has influenced the first is apparent from the slogan of the National Conference: " A State Park every Hundred Miles ". Now if the preservation of natural scenic beauty were the primary purpose for establishing parks, such scenic wonders are not to be found " every hundred miles ". This has been put succinctly by James L. Greenleaf:[2] " The fundamental and primary purpose in creating state parks is the preservation of natural scenic beauty. The emphasis on recreation is crowding out this purpose. ' A State park every hundred miles ', means that we are thinking in terms of the motor tourists and ugly tourist camps and not scenic wonders. Instead of this motto let us have ' a state park wherever nature smiles, a motor camp every hundred miles ' ".

Evidently the slogan was adopted to emphasize the need

[1] Torrey, Raymond H., *State Parks and Recreational Uses of State Forests in the United States*, 1926. National Conference on State Parks, Washington, D. C., 259 pp.

[2] Greenleaf, James L., " The Study and Selection of Sites for State Parks," *Landscape Architecture*, Boston, Mass., vol. xv, 1924-5, pp. 227-234.

for recreational areas within easy access of the people. It was aimed at creating a kind of popular enthusiasm for the movement which probably would not have followed on an appeal for the preservation of natural scenic beauty. While it is true that the National Conference is seeking to get away from this misleading slogan, it is nevertheless true that the movement has prospered because of its emphasis on the satisfaction of the public recreation needs. It is self-evident however that these same considerations cannot be applied to state forests. The primary purpose in their creation has been economic, that is, the conservation of timber and the preservation of the water supply. Recreation has entered as a secondary but important reason for their existence.

No division of this discussion has wider varieties of legislative provisions than this section on state parks. On the side of legislative and administrative control, the states vest authority in a park board (Arkansas, Kentucky, Texas, Utah); the forestry department (Georgia, New Hampshire, Oklahoma, South Carolina); or a combination of these two agencies (Virginia, Washington); department of public works (Idaho); the fish and game commission (Indiana, Louisiana, Michigan, Wisconsin, Iowa, New York, North Carolina, New Jersey, and Illinois). An effort was made by the National Conference to achieve some uniformity in state legislation by the appointment of a committee to draft a model park law. This committee found the difficulties so great that they got no further than making certain suggestions concerning what states might do to make their legislation more uniform. These suggestions called for the appointment of a state park board, to serve without pay, to have power to acquire, maintain and control state park areas, to grant concessions, to cooperate with city, county and federal agencies in the matter of parks and parkways, and to make any necessary surveys of the state looking toward the creation of new parks. The advantages of this report were that a number of the states adopted the proposals, thus bringing about a certain amount of uniformity. However, conditions within the states are so varied that different conditions have necessitated different procedures.

The most recent development in the legislation covering the administration of state parks and forests has been the consolidation of the various departments of the state government that had anything to do with either state parks or forests into a single governmental agency. This agency is usually called a conservation commission or board. Prior to this movement, in some of the states, several or all of the agencies mentioned above might have had some degree of supervision over these areas. The conservation commissions of Indiana, Michigan, Wisconsin, New Jersey and California are definite moves to centralize and coordinate the work of the various state agencies and to localize authority in one body. The laws of New York State provide for a similar commission to act in an advisory capacity to all of the state agencies having to do with the parks and reservations. As would be expected, the most progressive legislation has been adopted by those states where the park area is the greatest and where the need for centralization is most felt.

Not only on the question of administration is there wide diversity of legislative provision but also on the question of the acquisition and maintenance is there similar variety. Some states make direct appropriations (Connecticut, Iowa, Nebraska, Ohio, Tennessee, Wyoming). Others use revenues derived from fish and game licenses, occupation licenses and privilege taxes (Georgia, Kansas, Minnesota, Missouri, Pennsylvania, West Virginia). Still others partially support the system by concessions and rentals of camp sites (Idaho, Kansas, Massachusetts, Minnesota, Montana, New Hampshire, New Jersey, New York, North Carolina, Pennsylvania, Rhode Island, South Dakota, Texas, Vermont, Wisconsin). Indiana, Kentucky and Massachusetts derive varying degrees of support from charging admissions to parks and monuments. In the state of Washington, 75 per cent of the fines for the violation of the motor vehicle law goes for this purpose. California in 1927 passed a $6,000,000 bond issue for the purpose of purchasing sites for state parks. Oregon uses the state highway fund for its state parks. Indiana has provided by legislation for a two-mill tax for a period of seven years for the purchase of the Indiana Dunes Park.

These various types of acquisition and maintenance of State parks do not take into account one of the most fruitful means by which the states have acquired their park areas, namely, by gifts and donations. Most of Michigan's 60 parks and the 52 areas held by the State of Texas have been acquired in this way. Of approximately 6600 acres in the 21 state parks of Washington, 5900 acres have been donated to the state by private individuals or semi-public organizations. Some states have acquired park sites by the exchange of school lands for federally owned land which was suitable for park purposes.

No figures are available as to the extent to which the general public makes use of these 500 state parks and forests throughout the country. It is possible in a state like Indiana where an admission charge of ten cents is made to all park visitors to know accurately how many people visit them annually. The attendance at three of the parks in this state in 1926 was 142,541. In Missouri, where an effort is made to have all the visitors register, seven state parks had 19,929 registered visitors in 1927. The average number of daily campers in the California Redwood Camp is 500 for the entire season. From others of the states come, through their annual reports, estimates of the number of annual visitors.

The estimated attendance at the parks of Connecticut for the two-year period from Dec. 1, 1924 to Nov. 30, 1926 was: visitors, 1,580,728; campers, 67,055. Iowa reports that five of her state parks had an attendance of 600,000 visitors in 1926 and in the same year the visitors at the Michigan parks numbered more than two and a half millions. Minnesota estimates that 3,500,000 tourists visited her parks in the spring and summer of 1926. At two of Nebraska's state parks in 1927, the estimated attendance was 130,000.

However far these figures and estimates may be from the facts, they show that the public is making extensive use of these areas for recreational purposes. As has been said before, the automobile has made possible an extent of tourist travel heretofore unknown and the movement for state parks which is a phenomenon of the present time, is a movement to meet the needs of this touring populace. The number of permanent summer camping places in these reservations is also an indication that people living in urban areas are increasingly seeking the open country for their vacation periods.

On account of the wide diversity of the legislation on the subject of state parks and reservations, and on account of the extent of the legislation within each state, no attempt will be made here to embody examples of the legislation. Instead, a summary digest of the legislative provisions in each state will be included in Appendix D. This digest will include a statement of the number and acreage of the state parks and reservations in each state together with an analysis of the legislation grouped under the following categories:

(1) Administrative Agency.
(2) Powers and Duties of the Board.
(3) Semi-public or private organizations empowered to hold parks for the state.
(4) Methods of acquisition and maintenance.

FEDERAL PROVISIONS

The provisions that the federal government has made by legislation for public outdoor recreation cover such subjects as federal parks and monuments and federal forests. There are nineteen such parks under the administration of the National Park Service of the Department of the Interior, not including the recently created park in the Smoky Mountain Region of North Carolina and Tennessee. According to the 1925 report of the National Park Service,[1] there were 32 monuments under its control together with fourteen under the Department of Agriculture and ten administered by the War Department. There are more than 150 national forests having an aggregate acreage of 157 million acres.

Inasmuch as the National Park Service of the Department of the Interior is the federal agency having to do with the administration of most of the monuments and the national parks, its organization and work is of utmost importance to the student of federal activities. " Though the National Park Service is of recent origin, the system of national parks of which it is an outgrowth dates back half a century to the creation, 1872, of the Yellowstone National Park, the first true national park." [2] The national parks which had been created prior to 1916 numbered sixteen and were under the general supervision of the Department of the Interior. In that year, by legislative enactment,[3] a separate department was created within the Department of the Interior known as the National Park Service. Parts of that Act read as follows:

[1] U. S. Department of the Interior, Annual Report of the Director of the National Park Service, for fiscal year ended June 30, 1925, Govt. Printing Office, Washington, D. C.

[2] Cameron, Jenks, *The National Parks Service*, Service Monograph of the U. S. Government, No. 11, D. Appleton and Co., New York, 172 pp., 1922, p. 1.

[3] 39 Stat. 535.

That there is hereby created in the Department of the Interior a service to be called the National Park Service, which shall be under the charge of a director, who shall be appointed by the Secretary. . . . The service thus established shall promote and regulate the use of the Federal areas known as national parks, monuments, and reservations hereinafter specified by such means and measures as conform to the fundamental purpose of the said parks, monuments and reservations, which purpose is to conserve the scenery and the natural and historic objects and wild life therein and to provide for the enjoyment of the same in such manner and by such means as will leave them unimpaired for the enjoyment of future generations.

Sec. 2. That the director shall, under the direction of the Secretary of the Interior, have the supervision, management and control of the several national parks and national monuments which are now under the jurisdiction of the Department of the Interior. . . . Provided, that in the supervision, management and control of national monuments contiguous to national forests the Secretary of Agriculture may cooperate with said National Park Service to such extent as may be requested by the Secretary of the Interior.

Sec. 3. That the Secretary of the Interior shall make and publish such rules and regulations as he may deem necessary or proper for the use and management of the parks, monuments, and reservations under the jurisdiction of the National Park Service. . . . He may also grant privileges, leases and permits for the use of the land for the accommodation of visitors in the various parks, monuments or other reservations herein provided for, but for periods not exceeding twenty years. . . .

Sec. 4. (Provision for the making of rules and regulations).

The Director of the National Park Service, the Hon. Stephen T. Mather, in his annual reports notes the significance of the automobile in increasing the use that the public is making of these areas. The number of visitors to national parks and monuments increased from 811,516 in 1919 to 1,216,490 in 1922, and in 1925 that number had been increased to 2,108,084. In the creation of these national park areas, the major object has been to preserve places of incomparable scenic grandeur and beauty in their primitive naturalness. The fact that the standards set for a national park are very high, and that the government has not been liberal in the matter of appropriations for such purposes, accounts for the fact that the number of such areas is small.

The scenic supremacy of an area alone is not sufficient to gain it admission into the national park system. It must also be susceptible of whatever development is necessary to make it available for use by the millions of park visitors who may care to use it, without injuring in any way the extraordinary natural features which, under the expressed command of Congress, the National Park Service is to preserve, " unimpaired for the enjoyment of future generations ". Areas whose principal qualification is adaptability for recreational uses are not of course, of national park caliber.[1]

Thus, while the recreational advantages are uppermost in the minds of those promoting the national parks as to their usefulness, they are not the criteria by which an area is adjudged fitted for a national park.

Thus national parks are areas, preserved in their natural state, for the rest, recreation and education of the people. On the other hand, the national forests are " properties in a commercial sense, created to administer lumbering and grazing interests for the people ".[2] The national forests are under the administration of the Department of Agriculture, and while in them recreation is of secondary importance, it is by no means an unimportant use to which they are put. In these forests, " the Forest Service maintains 1500 camp-

[1] Mather, Stephen T., " Their ' Incomparable Scenic Grandeur ' ", *National Parks Bulletin*, Washington, D. C., November, 1927, p. 5.

[2] Work, Hubert, " The Official Policy Governing National Parks," *National Parks Bulletin*, Washington, D. C., May 26, 1925, pp. 14, 15.

ing grounds for tourists and local people ".[1] " Recreational use is not inconsistent with forest management but to the contrary a common by-product of such management." [2]

It is not to be inferred from this brief statement of the areas available for public recreation under federal governmental agencies, that the government is using very much of its public lands for recreational purposes.

More than 700,000 square miles of land within the boundaries of the States are owned and administered by the government . . . these 300,000 square miles are equipped with about 1600 recreation places. . . . Our nineteen National Parks . . . aggregate 11,372 square miles. . . . The truth is that the National Parks utilize well under two per cent . . . of the available public lands within the states; that the camp grounds in the National Forests are altogether inconsiderable; and that the Wild Life Refuges are recreational only in a special sense.   No wonder, with so vast and richly endowed a pleasure wilderness unutilized, that our one existing system, the National Parks is overwhelmed with demands for the admission of many areas which its special inhibitions make it impossible to accept.   Another recreational system without prohibitive conditions is one of the country's greatest needs.[3]

This recognition of the need for the federal government to do more in the way of providing facilities for public outdoor recreation has been expressed by others.   Robert Sterling Yard recommends the creation of a new system in the federal government to have power and money to provide for a recreational program and that alone.[4]   Barrington Moore

[1] *National Parks Bulletin* for April 30, 1924, "About Our Public Land."

[2] Sherman, E. A., " Outdoor Recreation on the National Forests," *Bulletin,* Forest Service, United States Department of Agriculture, 8 pp., p. 7.

[3] *National Parks Bulletin* for April 30, 1924, *op. cit.*

[4] Yard, Robert Sterling, " The Scenic Resources of the United States," *The Playground,* New York, vol. xviii, 1924-5, p. 214.

suggests a recreation commission of the government similar to the water-power commission with an advisory board of non-governmental persons.[1]   Henry V. Hubbard goes further in recommending that the federal government set up an Advisory Committee on Public Lands composed of the heads of the various departments or their subordinates, this committee to determine in a general way a broad policy concerning all the uses, primary and secondary, to which the lands might be put.[2]   One federal bureau having to do with the whole program of recreation in so far as the national government is concerned is the solution suggested by Joseph Hyde Pratt.[3]

That there should be a coordination of all the agencies which have anything to do with the federal supervision of recreation areas is obvious.   The National Park Service has charge of the national parks while the administration of the national monuments is divided among the National Park Service, the War Department and the Department of Agriculture.   The recreational facilities offered by the national forests come under the supervision of the Department of Agriculture.   Such a division of authority is plainly a lack of efficiency.   But before recommending that a separate commission or bureau be created, it is necessary to learn just whether or not the federal government should enter in a large way into the field of public recreation.   Under our governmental system, the tendency in the nineteenth century was toward decentralization of governmental functions.   If

---

[1] Moore, Barrington, " Outlines of a National Outdoor Recreational Policy with Special Reference to the Work of Federal Agencies," *The Playground*, New York, vol. xviii, 1924-5, p. 216.

[2] Hubbard, Henry V., " National Provision for the Enjoyment of our Scenic Resources," *The Playground*, New York, vol. xviii, 1924-5, p. 221, *et seq.*

[3] Pratt, Joseph Hyde, " Elements of a Federal Recreation Policy," *The Playground*, New York, vol. xviii, 1924-5, p. 225.

the tendency of the present century is toward greater centralization, and if the provision for public recreation belongs to
the functions of government, then it would seem as though
the most effective steps toward providing a coordinated
nation-wide system of public outdoor recreation could and
should be taken by the federal government.

BIBLIOGRAPHY

Annual Reports of the Director of the National Park Service, Department of the Interior, Government Printing Office, Washington.

Cammerer, Arno B., " Our National Parks, Their Present Status and
Service to the Public," *Parks and Recreation,* Rockford, Ill., vol.
viii, Jan.-Feb., 1925, pp. 185-202.

Greeley, W. B., " Recreation in the National Forests," *Review of Reviews,*
vol. 70, July, 1924, pp. 65-70.

Manning, Warren H., "A National Park System," *Parks and Recreation,*
vol. vii, 1923-24, p. 219.

Merriam, John C., " The Responsibility of Federal and State Governments for Recreation," *National Parks Bulletin,* Washington, D. C.,
March, 1926, pp. 5-8.

National Conference on City Planning, " State Plans and Planning
Agencies," *Bulletin 4,* New York, April, 1927.

National Park Service, *Glimpses of Our National Monuments,* U. S.
Department of Interior, Government Printing Office, 1926, 74 pp.

National Park Service, *Glimpses of Our National Parks,* U. S. Department of Interior, Government Printing Office, 1927, 62 pp.

Torrey, Raymond H., " State Parks Are Gaining Ground," *American
City,* New York, Jan., 1926, p. 63.

Waugh, Frank A., " Recreation in the National Forests," *National
Municipal Review,* New York, vol. xii, no. 6, June, 1923.

PART TWO
THE SOCIAL SIGNIFICANCE OF RECREATION

METHODOLOGY EMPLOYED IN PART TWO

" SUPERVISED Amusement Cuts Juvenile Crime by 96 per cent ", is the title of an article [1] which appeared several years ago in the *American City* magazine. In it, the author points out that in the neighborhood of Binghampton, New York, five years of supervised amusement had reduced juvenile crime by this startling figure. The implication from this report was that all that was needed to rid this and other regions of juvenile delinquency was to carry on an adequate system of recreation for the children. With this kind of superficial reasoning, this second part of this study will be concerned, together with an inductive method of attacking the problem of the association between supervised recreation and juvenile delinquency.

The justification for enacting legislation for public recreation, some indication of the extent of which may be seen from Part One of this study, is that recreation will promote order, safety, health, morals and general welfare of society. It may well do all of these things but how do we know that it does? No one has as yet demonstrated on objective grounds that the facts in the case show that the provision of recreation facilities does any one of these things. Recreation is " sold " to the public with the guarantee that these ends, or at least some of them, will be accomplished. It is not difficult to have laws passed or money raised to promote recreation when the plea is put forth in behalf of the children. But it is difficult to demonstrate that the social energy

---

[1] Engle, William I., " Supervised Amusement Cuts Juvenile Crime by 96%," *American City*, New York, Dec., 1919, pp. 515-517.

expended here is more wisely spent than for some other common good.

To arrive objectively at an answer to the question of whether or not the provision for public recreation promotes the general welfare of society will require a large number of studies. The field will have to be broken up into small sections for analysis. One small segment was chosen for investigation here, namely, the problem of the association, if any exists, between the presence of recreation areas and the occurrence of juvenile delinquency. The study will be preceded by a statement of the various methods that have been employed to evaluate the significance of recreation in relation to this social situation. These methods are set forth in the succeeding chapter together with a statement of their inadequacy to answer the question. The final chapter will be concerned with the results of the analysis made of Manhattan Island to determine the extent to which the presence or absence of play areas is associated with the presence or absence of juvenile delinquency.

The most glaring fallacy into which the writers and investigators mentioned in the following chapter fall is that of assigning to the presence or absence of recreation facilities the chief contributing cause to the production of delinquency. If this were not true, it would hardly seem necessary to say that human conduct is the result of many causes. When a boy breaks into a cellar for the purpose of stealing, society wants to know the whole mental and environmental history of the child in order if possible to ascertain the reason for his act. Is he weak mentally due to hereditary defects? Has he come from a shattered home and consequently lacked early training? Has he learned his anti-social conduct from criminal parents or bad companions? Has his school training been defective in failing to enlist his interests in constructive activities? If a child of foreign-born parents, is this offense to be explained on the basis of a conflict of cultures? These are only a few of the possible reasons for the delinquency. They are sufficient, however, for us to conclude that any statement to the effect that the crime would have been prevented by the presence of supervised recreation facilities is thoroughly inaccurate. That the presence of such facilities might have engaged the boy's attention and prevented the offense is within reason.

Herein lies the difficulty in the scientific study of any social situation. There are so many possible causes, let us call them factors, which may account for human responses. The chemist in the laboratory is able to experiment with the chemical elements he wishes to combine while preventing the factors of temperature, etc., and other chemical elements from interfering with his analysis. But the social scientist is unable to control his experiments so as to hold constant the factors which he does not want to consider. His solution lies in endeavoring to measure the association between two factors which he is studying while the other factors remain the same.

The two factors in this analysis which we desire to relate are the presence of play areas in Manhattan and the amount of juvenile delinquency. No attempt was made to deal with the hereditary history or the psychological background of the children studied. Only factors in the environment were taken into consideration. Recognizing the importance of the former factors, it would be unscientific to arrive at a mathematical statement of the association between the factors related, knowing that we have omitted a significant group of factors. With regard to the environment, certain situations had to be excluded because of insufficient data, namely, the presence of docks, wharves, railroads, etc., the economic status of the population, and the effects of religious and social welfare agencies. The things that were studied were:

the existence of supervised play areas, the incidence of juvenile delinquency, the racial composition of the population, the child density per acre, and the uniformity of police regulation. After the first two of these had been related, evidence was collected covering the last three in order to determine if the conclusions reached on the first comparisons were sound. In other words, an effort was made to hold the factors of racial composition, child density, and police regulation constant while comparisons were being made between the factors of recreation areas and juvenile delinquency.

The merit claimed for this method is not that it settles the question but that it takes into account more of the factors which are generally supposed to contribute to the production of delinquency, than has been the case with previous studies. This analysis is in the nature of a scientific exploration endeavoring to gather together all the evidence, for which the data are available, either to prove or disprove the assertion that the provision of recreational facilities will result in a reduction of juvenile crime.

CHAPTER VI

ATTEMPTS TO EVALUATE RECREATION IN RELATION TO JUVENILE DELINQUENCY

THE cost to society of enacting the large amount of legislation in the field of public recreation cannot be measured. And it is equally difficult to estimate the amount of money that is being spent in carrying into effect this legislation. In 1927, the cities reporting to the Playground and Recreation Association[1] as having a supervised recreation program spent approximately $32,000,000. Westchester County in New York State, which has been a leader in the development of a county-wide program, has spent, in the first five years of its work, more than $40,000,000.[2] While the federal and state governments have not spent proportionately large public funds, the value of gifts by individuals and organizations for state and federal parks would run into hundreds of millions of dollars. To this national expenditure must be added the budgets of such promotive agencies as the Playground and Recreation Association of America, the Recreation Department of the Russell Sage Foundation, the National Conference on State Parks, the National Conference on Outdoor Recreation, and similar organizations.

It may be that this large expenditure of social energy is justified in terms of the promotion of the general welfare. At least, it is defended on this basis. But the defense usually rests on opinions and assumptions rather than on careful in-

[1] *The Playground*, New York, *Year Book*, April, 1928.

[2] *Report of the Westchester County Park Commission*, April 30, 1927, Rand, McNally and Co., New York, p. 8.

vestigation of the facts.   It is one thing to say, as Eugene
T. Lies does,[1] that " two-thirds of our school children are
physically defective ", it is quite another thing to demonstrate that a program of public recreation, adequately supervised, is going to improve that condition.   It is not difficult
to make such statements as that which appeared in the *New
Orleans Item* for February 4, 1923, which says : [2]

The number of children in New Orleans who are physically fit
has more than doubled since 1918, Mr. di Benedetto pointed out.
Physical tests in that year showed only 23.6 per cent of the
children examined to be normal.   In 1922, following five years
of playground work, this percentage had increased to 50.5 per
cent, according to the annual reports of the Playground Commission.

Granting that playgrounds may have had some influence on
this general rise in public health, have they been the chief
cause, or have many other conditions changed in New
Orleans in those five years to account for this improvement ?

Such aprioristic statements with regard to the effect of
recreation on health could be paralleled with statements of
its effects on other aspects of the general welfare.   They are
frequently made with respect to the influence of recreation
on juvenile delinquency, the subject-matter of our present
investigation.   These statements together with other
methods of attacking the problem of the relation between
recreation and delinquency are now to be considered.

Evidence from the Experience of Community Officials.—
The easiest but most unreliable answer to the question of
whether or not supervised play influences the amount of

[1] Lies, Eugene T., " Play and the Well-Being of the Child," *Hospital
Social Service Quarterly*, March, 1925, pp. 165-172, p. 172.

[2] " Playgrounds Cause Child Crime Wane," *New Orleans Item*, New
Orleans, La., Feb. 4, 1923.

juvenile delinquency is found by taking the experience of leaders in communities which have adopted a recreation program. Such testimony, if uncritically accepted, might lead one to believe that delinquency resulted solely from lack of playgrounds. From the standpoint of the social scientist this condition, if true, would be very gratifying. William I. Engle in recounting the work done in the neighborhood of Binghamton, New York,[1] says: " Supervised playgrounds, parks, amusements, manual labor classes and boys' clubs have in five years reduced juvenile crime and delinquency 96 per cent in the industrial center of the southern portion of New York State, according to figures recently compiled by the Broome County Humane Society and Relief Association."

Several years ago, the Playground and Recreation Association gathered from various centers testimonies regarding the value of a recreation program. Sections from that bulletin [2] read:

Since playgrounds were started in Knoxville, Tenn., City Manager Brownlow of that city claims that juvenile delinquency has decreased 50%. In Toronto in a district of 50,000 people which sent 30% of the total of child delinquents to the juvenile court, delinquency was reduced to practically nil within one year of the organization of a boys' group by the Toronto Rotary Club. . . . The probation officer in Visalia, Cal., claims a reduction of 80% in juvenile delinquency since the organization of the community recreation system. . . . The annual report of the Division of Parks and Recreation of the Department of Public Welfare of St. Louis, Mo., contains the following statement: " A comparison of the number of juvenile delinquents in the effective area of every playground in St. Louis in 1917, with

[1] Engle, William I., *op. cit.*

[2] Playground and Recreation Association of America, " Recreation Reduces Crime," *Bulletin 1294*, New York, December 18, 1925.

the number of delinquents in 1921 in the same respective area, showed a decrease of fifty per cent. In the four playgrounds established in 1916, the number of juvenile delinquents in 1917 in their respective undeveloped playground area, as compared with the same area in 1921 (three years after the establishment of the playgrounds), shows a decrease in every instance of 75%."

Just as striking experiences are reported from other centers. The Mayor of Memphis, Tenn., is quoted as follows:[1] " In the communities where there are playgrounds, where healthful sports are encouraged, the morality of the boys is high — not a boy was taken into the juvenile court this year from the neighborhood where there is a playground." " Chief of Police Conlon of Leominster,[2] Mass., says that delinquency cases in Leominster averaged ninety-one a year prior to the organization of Community Service, the local recreation agency. Since its coming, the number decreased to fifty-three in 1923." " We find [3] New Orleans today, with 13 playgrounds, showing less juvenile delinqency than in 1909, although the city has increased in population over 60,000 in this period." " From Bluefield, West Virginia,[4] which used to send, on an average, approximately 50 boys a year to the state reformatory, came a report that during the last three years, when the city has had under competent direction playgrounds and a boys' club, only two cases have been given over to the reformatory."

The statement of L. H. Weir when he was chief probation officer of Cincinnati is a little more conservative:[5]

[1] " Finds Investment in Youth Pays the Community Well," Prince Albert, Saskatchewan, *Daily Herald* for Feb. 6, 1925.

[2] " Money is Spent for Kiddies' Play," Des Moines, Iowa *Capital*, April 17, 1924.

[3] *New Orleans Item, op. cit.*

[4] " Supervised Play Cuts Delinquency," *Christian Science Monitor*, April 17, 1924.

[5] " Plea for More Playgrounds to Prevent Abolishing Children," New York *Times*, Nov. 26, 1922.

In 1906 there were 1748 children legally before the Juvenile court. . . . Of these, 1450 were delinquents. In the fall of that year a beginning was made in opening playgrounds in the downtown portions of the city. In the year just closed there were 993 delinquent children before the court. Each year has noted a marked decrease. While some of this decrease may be due to other causes, the work of the court for instance, we are perfectly sure that one of the main factors has been the opportunity afforded the thousands of children in the most congested districts of the city to play in a natural and spontaneous manner.

Such testimonies as these could be multiplied. The sweeping generalizations which are characteristic of all of them must be viewed with caution. If taken at their face value they would seem to imply that the provision of play areas will, by some occult legerdemain, overcome all the factors of defective heredity, shattered homes, bad companions, and the dozen other contributing causes which Healy [1] and Burt [2] have found go toward the making of a delinquent. It is not a question of whether or not the facts as stated are correct. It is rather a problem of the interpretation of the facts. It is entirely wrong to ascribe the reduction in the amount of delinquency in a given locality to the introduction of a recreation program unless it is known that all the other factors in the given situation remained constant. Mr. Weir's statement may well be called conservative in that he recognized that the change in court procedure was one element in the decrease in delinquency cases. He might have found on examination that in 1922 as compared with 1906 many other changes had taken place in Cincinnati, all of which might have had some bearing on the amount of juvenile delinquency.

[1] Healy, William, *The Individual Delinquent*, Little, Brown and Co., Boston, 1915, 830 pp.

[2] Burt, Cyril, *The Young Delinquent*, D. Appleton and Co., New York, 1925, 619 pp.

To interpret a social situation in the light of one factor only without taking into consideration changes in other variables is liable to give rise to a very faulty interpretation of cause and effect.

Evidence from Map Studies. — Perhaps equally inconclusive and yet indicating a more critical analytical approach to the problem have been certain map studies. The technique here used was to make a map of the city showing the location of the play areas and then, on the same map, by means of dots or beaded pins to locate the addresses of the juvenile delinquents. Mr. T. P. Eslick, Chief Juvenile Officer of the District Court of Iowa located at Des Moines, made such a map of Des Moines. He found that delinquency dropped off in proportion to proximity to the play areas. Of his study he says:[1] " These maps fully convinced me. My ten years' experience in juvenile courts in Denver and Des Moines have made me a firm believer in the proposition that playgrounds pay large dividends to the taxpayer in that they prevent much delinquency which would be a very expensive proposition from the standpoint of both dollars and citizenship."

T. Earl Sullenger[2] reports the result of his study as follows:

We are safe in saying that a majority of children who are brought into court get there because they have been in search of pleasure. . . . In order to make a complete study of the relation of recreation to delinquency in Omaha, it seemed best to ascertain from which districts of the city the delinquent children who were before the court during 1922 and 1923 had come. A simple method of determining how far any special neighborhood was furnishing the court with cases, was to locate accur-

[1] *Playground and Recreation Association of America, op. cit.*

[2] Sullenger, T. Earl, " Summary of a Study of the Juvenile Delinquent in Omaha," Univ. of Omaha *Bull.*, vol. i, no. 5, Omaha, Neb.

ately by street numbers on a map of the city each family which had furnished the court with one or more delinquent children. It was found that 88% of the homes were located more than one-half mile from the nearest playground. . . . This map also shows that the greatest amount of delinquency occurs in the most congested sections of the city and especially in the regions near the railroad tracks and the river.

A third map of this type was made by the Playground and Community Service Commission of New Orleans.[1] The evidence here was just as conclusive. A practically spotless area surrounded each playground, shading off into greater and greater density in proportion to the distance from a playground. The influence of thoroughfares was likewise noted, indicating that children apparently did not cross wide thoroughfares to reach a playground even though the playground bordered on such a street.

To test the validity of this type of analysis the author spotted on a map of Manhattan the addresses of 1795 boys brought into the Children's Court in 1926. On the same map he placed the park playgrounds. The radius of effectiveness of a play area for children fifteen years and younger is usually considered to be one-quarter mile. How that figure has been arrived at will be discussed later. The areas of densest concentration of spots were:

1. The lower East Side, below 14th Street
2. The West Side, from 46th to 63rd Streets, west of Eighth Avenue
3. The upper East Side, above 96th Street, east of Lexington Avenue
4. The Harlem District

Using each of six playgrounds as a center, circles one-half

[1] "Play Plant Gifts Are Needed Here," New Orleans, La. *Times Picyune*, April 22, 1923.

mile in diameter were drawn. Then, for purposes of comparison, other one-half mile circles were drawn, bordering as nearly as possible on the former circles and not containing either within or on their borders a playground.

The procedure followed for comparing these areas was simply that of counting the number of dots falling within the contiguous circles the former of which contained a play area, while the latter embraced no such area. In the circle of which the DeWitt Clinton playground was the center there were 21 cases, while in that just to the east of this play area there were 40 cases. Mount Morris Park had a total of 36 cases, while the region to the north of it contained 41 dots. The Tompkins Square playground area contained 57, while the circle whose rough borders were Delancey, East 4th, Bowery and Suffolk included 76. The Seward Park district had only 46, whereas the section bounded by Lafayette, Allen, Canal and Prince streets contained a total of 52. However, the reverse was true of the Hudson Park area as compared with the circle embraced within Macdougal, Lafayette, Canal and West Houston streets. The former had 45 dots while the latter had only 25. The same situation was found in the Thomas Jefferson Park district when placed alongside of the area lying between 118th and 128th streets, east of Third avenue. Fifty-four cases appeared in the former while there were only 41 in the latter.

More districts would have been compared but for the difficulty of getting contiguous areas, one of which had a playground and one of which did not, and yet both of which had a sufficient number of cases to reduce to a minimum the element of chance. Suffice it to say that on the counts made and the comparisons elicited, the evidence from such a map study far from corroborates the rather positive and conclusive results attained by the investigations previously mentioned. While it is true that four of the six districts show a higher number of arrests in the areas outside the circle of effectiveness of the playground, the difference is not great enough to be conclusive. Especially is this true in the absence of knowledge of the other factors in the situation, such as, nationality groupings, density of population, settlement-house activities, the economic status of the population, and other factors. It might be contended that by taking contiguous areas these factors would remain constant, but that such is hardly the case will appear later. The best that can be said from this evidence is that while there might be a connection between the location of play areas and the number of juvenile delinquents, if Manhattan be typical and if we have sufficient cases, yet we cannot say conclusively that juvenile delinquency tends to increase as we move away from play areas.

Over against the conclusions drawn from the studies in Omaha, Des Moines and New Orleans, stands the study made by Joseph W. Sanford, Chief Probation Officer of Washington, D. C. He made a map of that city similar to the ones made in these other centers. He found a clustering of cases of delinquents in the areas nearest to the playgrounds. The result reached by Mr. Sanford was quite at variance from that arrived at by the investigation of the United States Children's Bureau, which found that " in general those (areas) having the poorest play facilities also had the greatest amount of juvenile delinquency." [1]

Evidence from Case Studies.—A third type of approach to this problem is that of the case method. This is illustrated by the Report of the Joint Committee on Negro Child Study in New York City.[2] This committee made an investigation

---

[1] " Playgrounds Fail to Halt Juvenile Crime, Map Shows," *Washington Star*, August 17, 1925.

[2] *A Study of Delinquent and Neglected Negro Children before the New York City Children's Court*, Joint Committee on Negro Child Study in New York City, 1927, 48 pp.

of the delinquent and neglected children brought before the New York City Children's Court in 1925. Five hundred and forty-three or about eight and one-half per cent of the total number of children brought before the court in that year were Negro children. Of 50 cases selected at random from these, " the lack of opportunities for supervised recreation showed up conspicuously. In only one instance was there any statement on the part of the child or its parents that it belonged to any club or had any contact with organized recreation. The one boy who had such a contact was a member of a Boy Scout troop." Of the findings of this committee, no. 6 is interesting: " Contributory causes of juvenile delinquency among Negro children, the Committee found to be: 1. Lack of opportunities for supervised recreation." Of the recommendations these are noteworthy: " 2. That with regard to recreation there be: (a) A coordinated all-year-round recreation program in colored districts, (d) An increase in municipal facilities for play."

In the report of the director, Henry W. Thurston, of a survey of juvenile delinquency made in Rochester, New York, 64 cases were studied.[1] The object in view in the survey was to find out what could be done to further prevent delinquency in that city. By a concentrated study of these cases, the survey staff made an effort to show what social agencies were at work to aid the delinquent and his family. " It should be an especially challenging fact to social workers dealing with these delinquent children to note that in at least 32 out of 64 families the parents were found not to have an appreciation of the worth of supervised recreation and apparently make no attempt to provide safe and wholesome recreation for their children, either within the home or

[1] Thurston, Henry W., " Condensed Report of a Survey of Juvenile Delinquency in Rochester, New York," *Bulletin No. 9*, Aug., 1923, Child Welfare League of America, New York, 44 pp., p. 7.

from the resources of the community outside the home." As a part of this study, a chart was made to show the instances of harmful and of destructive use of spare time. On this chart, improper use of an amusement park is mentioned at least eleven times, six of these also involving improper use of automobiles; poolrooms and misuse of movies, seventeen times; street corners, twenty-five times; gangs, twelve times. As helpful influences to the boys in the use of their spare time, clubs were mentioned in seven instances, playgrounds in five, parks in four, and the church in thirteen.

Edith Abbott and Sophonisba P. Breckinridge [1] report the results of an inquiry to show the character of the Chicago neighborhoods from which the juvenile delinquents had come during the first ten years of the establishment of the children's court. They found the greatest number from the west side, the congested wards lying along the river and the canals, together with the industrial sections and the stockyards. Here also, they found the poorest families, living under the most unsanitary conditions, and ignorant.

It is, of course, especially characteristic of the poor and congested wards of the city that they have few parks and playgrounds; and in no other group of homes are the private facilities for recreation so slight as in these crowded tenement quarters. To test the extent to which the delinquent child was also a " child without play " a count was made of the number of boys in the special year, 1903-1904, who did not live within accessible distance, that is, within half a mile, of any public place of recreation. The homes of 832 of these boys were located and it was found that only 449 of them, or 54 per cent of the total number, had opportunities for recreation or play.

Evidence from Other Studies.—In 1907 Allen T. Burns,

---

[1] Abbott, Edith, and Breckinridge, Sophonisba P., " The Delinquent Child and the Home," Charities Publication Committee, New York, 1912, 354 pp., ch. ix, pp. 151-159.

who was then Dean of the Chicago School of Civics and Philanthropy, attacked the problem of getting a measure of the association between playgrounds and juvenile delinquency.[1] His approach was similar to the map studies mentioned above except that by taking a period of years, 1899 to 1907, he was able to get a check on his results. In addition, his method included case studies for one of the years. Ninety per cent of the cases for the first, fifth and eighth years were charted upon city maps by different colored tacks. In addition, all the cases for the year 1903-1904 were personally traced. The " successful cases ", that is, those qualified for release from the jurisdiction of the court, were plotted on the same maps. With respect to his study of these cases, he found that whereas for the city as a whole, 39 per cent of the cases were successful, the proportion of successful cases within one mile of each of the six large parks was 46 per cent. In the matter of municipal playgrounds, between the years 1900 and 1907, the radius of efficiency of one-quarter mile from each playground showed a decrease of juvenile delinquency of 24 per cent as compared with 18 per cent for the city as a whole. The small parks of the South Side showed an even more startling association. Whereas in the first five years of the court, this area provided 40 per cent of the juvenile cases of the entire city, two years after the opening of the small parks and at the end of the eighth year of the court's work, the South Side furnished only 34 per cent of the city's juvenile offenders. In those two years the rate of delinquency in the South Side decreased 17 per cent, while for the city as a whole it increased 12 per cent.

Cyril Burt [2] has arrived at a mathematical statement of

---

[1] Burns, Allen T., " Relation of Playgrounds to Juvenile Delinquency," *Charities and Commons*, October 3, 1908. See *Bull. 385*, Playground and Recreation Ass'n. of America, New York, Jan. 28, 1921.

[2] Burt, Cyril, *op. cit.*, p. 149 and footnote p. 150.

the association between recreation spaces and delinquency. He says:

In almost every quarter in London, the incidence of crime is high in areas most remote from open spaces, where there are no parks, playing fields, or recreation grounds. The correlation between the percentage of young offenders and the amount of open space per acre of land was—.22. A similar correspondence between the absence of open spaces and the presence of juvenile crime has been noted in a survey carried out at Liverpool by Mr. F. J. Marquis, formerly Warden of the Liverpool University Settlement.

The difficulty, however, with these studies is that Mr. Burt gives no indication of the methods by which the results were obtained or the data upon which they were based. In order to interpret the conclusions, it would be necessary to know these facts.

These four types of studies have this in common, that they all find a significant degree of association between the presence of supervised recreation areas and the absence of juvenile delinquency. *A priori,* it would seem to be a valid contention, inasmuch as it is certainly true that when a child is playing under leadership he is not stealing " junk " or breaking into cellars. But the most careful of the above investigations are those which do not claim too much for recreation. The trouble with most of the recreation enthusiasts is that they find in the provision of recreation spaces a panacea for too many social evils. No city executive would refuse to go to any length to supply a playground in a congested section of his locality if he were satisfied that by its provision delinquency would be eliminated from that district. On the other hand, no sensible recreation leader would make such a contention if he is at all cognizant of the many factors that contribute to the making of the criminal.

At the present time (April, 1928) there is a study in progress, by the Illinois Institute of Juvenile Research, of the problem of juvenile delinquency in Chicago. An effort is being made to compare neighborhoods in different years to see what changes have taken place in the amount of delinquency coming from these sections. These changes are being related to other changes, such as, racial composition of the population, recreational opportunities, presence of railroad yards, canals, industries, etc. Mr. Clifford Shaw of this Institute told the author that they had found that the placing of a playground in a neighborhood had, in some cases, apparently brought about a reduction in the amount of delinquency, while in other cases the reverse was true. This merely corroborates the fact that in dealing with juvenile crime, a large number of factors must be taken into account. Even a casual reading of the conclusions of Healy based on a study of 1000 " repeaters " with regard to the causative factors in the production of delinquency, i.e., defective mentality, bad home conditions, bad companions, hereditary defects, poor environment, etc., leads one naturally to be skeptical about any study which finds that by making one element in the environment better that alone will solve the problem. Healy would say that recreation areas under adequate supervision are certainly to be reckoned as one element in the situation. Concerning them, he says: [1]

A public playground is no incentive towards good conduct unless better mental activities and better mental content are fostered there. . . . We have been exceedingly impressed by what we have learned concerning the paucity of mental interests of individuals who start criminalistic careers. . . . These unfortunate individuals are generally unaccustomed to playing games that have interesting mental content, they rarely are found to read the type of books which lead them into constructive activi-

[1] Healy, Wm., *op. cit.*, pp. 284, 297.

ties. They have, almost universally, very slight knowledge of the modern scientific interests, such as electricity, which fairly possess the minds of more fortunate young people. Such normal activities as that of collecting objects are rarely met with.

Healy may be correct. The playground in itself may not be a factor in preventing anything. Unless wholesome activities are fostered there under competent leadership, it might well be a means of propagating delinquency. On a tour of the play areas in Manhattan made on April 12, 1928, the author found in a remote corner of Mount Morris Park ten boys, ranging in age from about 9 to 18 years, shooting " craps ". Here was an instance, certainly, of the play area offering an opportunity for the meeting place of boys bent on other than wholesome activities. It would be a highly interesting and profitable study to find out to what extent the presence of open spaces, without adequate supervision, offers facilities for the meeting of gangs and the fostering of crime.

If the contention be a valid one that the methods of attack used in the investigations outlined in this chapter are faulty in that they would place too much emphasis on the single factor of recreation, then the way is open for a study which avoids this evil. If it were possible to get the data on all the factors which contribute to the making of a delinquent, it might be possible to arrive at a mathematical statement which would approximately represent the place of recreation in such a whole. But the data are not available. The best that can be done is to take into account all the factors for which data are available and which are generally supposed to be contributing factors in the environmental causation of delinquency. Such a procedure has been followed with the results as set forth in the succeeding chapter.

BIBLIOGRAPHY

Addams, Jane, *The Spirit of Youth and the City Streets*, The Macmillan Co., 1910, 162 pp.

Cooley, Edwin J., *Probation and Delinquency*, Catholic Charities of the Archdiocese of New York, New York, 1927, 544 pp.

Doeblin, Maud I., " Recreation *versus* Delinquency," *School and Society*, Garrison, New York, vol. xii, Nov. 20, 1920, pp. 478-487.

Kirchwey, George W., " Crime Waves and Crime Remedies," *The Survey Graphic*, New York, March 1, 1926, pp. 593 *et seq.*

Lies, Eugene T., "Juvenile Delinquency and Recreation," *The Playground*, vol. xviii, 1924-5, pp. 457-460.

National Child Labor Committee, Child Welfare in Kentucky, New York, National Child Labor Committee, 1919.

Platt, Charles, " Leisure as a Cause or Cure of Crime," *American City*, December, 1926, pp. 863-869.

Slawson, John, *The Delinquent Boy*, R. G. Badger, Boston, 1926, 477 pp.

Thrasher, Frederic M., *The Gang, A Study of 1313 Gangs in Chicago*, University of Chicago Press, Chicago, 1927, 571 pp.

U. S. Department of Labor, Children's Bureau, Dependent and Delinquent Children in North Dakota and South Dakota, No. 160, Washington, D. C., Oct. 22, 1926.

U. S. Department of Labor, Children's Bureau, Dependent and Delinquent Children in Georgia, No. 161, Washington, D. C., Oct. 22, 1926.

CHAPTER VII

ASSOCIATION BETWEEN PLAY AREAS AND DELINQUENCY IN MANHATTAN

THE author makes no claim that the subsequent analysis lays to rest the question of whether or not there is any association between the presence of play space and the incidence of juvenile delinquency. This study is in the nature of an exploration to discover, if possible, what the environmental factors are that contribute to the making or the preventing of delinquency. In so far as he has taken into account several variables, he does maintain that the method followed is sounder scientifically than the methods discussed in the previous chapter. The hope of any student of the social sciences is that, even though his conclusions may be seriously questioned, his method may admit of further enlargement and experimentation which will eventually lead to more adequate results.

The question involved is more than simply the problem of whether or not there is any association between play space and juvenile delinquency. The lower East Side of Manhattan supplies as many as one-third to one-fourth of the total number of cases coming annually before the Children's Court of that island. And yet the lower East Side appears to be pretty well dotted with play areas: Tompkins Square, Seward Park, Corlears Hook, Seventh Ward Athletic Field at Cherry and Clinton Streets, Hamilton Fish Park, Coleman Oval at Cherry and Market Streets, to say nothing of the vacation-school playgrounds and the after-school athletic centers. Such a superficial examination of the facts leads, however, to an unjustified conclusion. Of the 320,514 children, 5 to 15 years old living in Manhattan, 82,832, or 25.8 per cent, live in this section of the city. The problem is not, How many play areas are there in a given district and how many arrests for delinquency come from that district? but it is rather, Is there any relation between the amount of play space per child in a given area and the proportion of arrests to the total child population of the same area?

To test for the presence or absence of this association was the purpose of this investigation. Two measures were to be compared. The first of these was a measure of the amount of play space in use per child and the second was the proportion of arrests for delinquency to the total child population. In order to make use of the 1920 census figures for the population of Manhattan, it was necessary to take the play areas in use in 1920 and also the arrests for delinquency in that year. When the term play area is used here, it is understood to mean play spaces under supervision and not merely open spaces which may or may not be used for play.

In order to get a geographical unit smaller than the island as a whole, it was essential to divide the entire area under consideration into districts. Whereas the island as a whole was too large, the sanitary districts as units were too small, comprising as they do approximately 43 acres. In the definition of the unit, three considerations were taken into account. It was advisable to get areas bounded by thoroughfares on the hypothesis that children tend not to cross thoroughfares to reach a play space. In addition, the area should constitute reasonable uniformity with regard to racial composition. And only reasonable uniformity can be reached in this respect, as it is possible to travel only a few blocks on the lower East Side and pass from a neighborhood largely Italian to one principally Russian. A final consideration was to define the unit in such a way that it would embrace the area of effectiveness of a neighborhood playground on the assumption that a play space were located in the centre. As has been said before, children will travel one-quarter to one-half mile to a neighborhood playground. In round numbers the area of such a circle would be 400 acres.

With these three considerations in mind, Manhattan was divided into 28 districts. In order to distinguish them in this report from the sanitary districts, they will be called play districts. Inasmuch as the population figures were obtained from the sanitary districts, the boundaries of these play districts had to coincide with the boundaries of the sanitary districts. The irregularities of the boundaries are to be accounted for largely on the basis of the boundary characteristics of the sanitary districts. Other such irregularities are to be explained by taking into account the fact that these areas are fairly homogeneous as to population and for the most part surrounded by thoroughfares. The play districts were numbered from 1 to 28, beginning at the lower extremity of the island as shown on the map on page 145.

AN INDEX OF DELINQUENCY

The next step in the procedure was to take the data with regard to the children arraigned for delinquency from the records of the Children's Court for 1920. The cases came under three broad classifications: 1. Delinquent Child; 2. Neglected Child; and 3. Special Mental Proceedings. Only those falling under the first category were taken, since the Neglected Child is one whose parents have failed to take care of it, and the child who comes under the case of Special Mental Proceedings is one who is known to have some mental defect which accounts for the delinquency. It is not to be understood that all of the delinquent cases are without mental defects. The probabilities are that a great many of them are suffering from such defects. However, it is difficult to get the necessary affidavits from physicians to the effect that the child has a mental defect and hence it is highly probable that children with pronounced mental deficiencies are included in the classification, Delinquent Child.   For all of the cases falling within this class, this information was taken: a. Address; b. Date of Arrest; c. Age; d. Sex; e. Color; f. Nativity of Child and Parents; g. Character of Offense.

Then these cases, numbering 3304, were distributed according to address among the 28 play districts of the island and counted.   From the population figures of New York City [1] was taken the child population, 7 to 15 years old, of each of the sanitary districts.   In order to reduce these sanitary district figures for population to totals for the play districts, the numbers for the sanitary districts making up each play district were simply added together.   In order to arrive at a proportion which would represent the relation between the arrests for delinquency and the total population of each play district, the number of arrests in each case was divided by the total number of children, 7 to 15 years old, living in that play district.   This multiplied by 1,000 gave a figure which we shall call the delinquency index, as shown in the last column of Table 1 on the next page.

AN INDEX OF ADEQUACY OF PLAY SPACE

In order to compare this index of delinquency with the amount of play space in use in 1920 in each of the 28 districts, it was necessary to arrive at some index of play space. It was not sufficient to get a figure which would represent the relationship between the number of children in the district and the amount of the play space.   It was important, rather, to discover whether or not the amount of play space

[1] *Statistical Sources for Demographic Studies of Greater New York, 1920*, New York City 1920 Census Committee, Inc., edit. by Walter Laidlaw.

TABLE 1. INDEX OF DELINQUENCY BY PLAY DISTRICTS OF MANHATTAN, 1920

Play Dist.	Child Pop.	Arrests	$\dfrac{\text{Arrests}}{\text{Child Pop.}} \times 1,000$
1	1,760	42	23.9
2	18,508	232	12.5
3	30,102	281	9.3
4	34,222	301	8.8
5	12,217	211	17.3
6	10,683	148	13.9
7	5,276	73	13.8
8	3,631	42	11.6
9	9,428	126	13.4
10	9,740	87	8.9
11	6,377	117	18.3
12	11,977	181	15.1
13	1,664	13	7.8
14	5,770	19	3.3
15	14,947	116	7.8
16	21,742	128	5 9
17	4,427	41	9.3
18	9,097	58	6.4
19	7,114	37	5.2
20	29,603	234	7.9
21	26,323	346	13.1
22	7,889	102	12.9
23	10,384	201	19.4
24	8,556	81	9.5
25	8,147	30	3.7
26	4,617	32	6.9
27	4,721	18	3.8
28	1,592	6	3.7

in use was adequate to meet the needs of the children living in a given district. What was desired then was not merely an index of play space but rather an index of the adequacy of play areas. For example, if we say there are 1,000 children living in a neighborhood and we regard 300 square feet per child as an adequate amount of outdoor recreation space, then the area needed in that neighborhood would be 300,000 square feet. Suppose there is in use in the section 100,000 square feet of space, then the measure of the adequacy of the play areas in use would be .333.

To arrive at a figure which would represent for each of the 28 play districts such an index of adequacy, a method was employed similar to that used by Charles J. Storey of the Recreation Department of the Russell Sage Foundation.[1] In order to compute this percentage, three things must be known: (1) the number of children; (2) the amount of space required per child; and (3) the number of children who will want to play at any one time. The first is known. The latter two involve standards about which there is more or less of agreement among recreation leaders. The amount of space required per child depends on the age and sex of the child. For boys up to nine years and girls up to fifteen, Mr. Storey found that 100 square feet is adequate to allow for swings, slides, game boards, basketball, and other types of games. For indoor baseball, football, and other group games not requiring a large amount of space, 250 square feet per child would be sufficient. For outdoor baseball and similar sports requiring a large amount of space, 1000 square feet would be necessary. For the group with which this study has to do, boys and girls from seven to fifteen years old, 300 square feet per child might be said to come near to meeting the needs of all ages involved.

[1] Hanmer, Lee F., *Public Recreation, a Study of Parks, Playgrounds and Other Outdoor Recreation Facilities, Regional Survey*, vol. v, Regional Plan of New York and Its Environs, New York, 1928, 256 pp.

Taking 300 square feet per child, the next question to be answered is, How many children in a given neighborhood will want to play at any one time? It is obvious that many children get their recreation in other ways than by outdoor activity. Many will be engaged at least some of their leisure time out of school in work, others will prefer to roam the streets or to play in the streets, no matter how adequate the play space. In addition to these considerations, not all of the children will want to play at any one time. In order to determine how many children in a given neighborhood do play at one time, Mr. Storey, as part of the report mentioned above, made a number of counts of children using the play areas. On nine of these areas — Hudson, Five Points, Rutger's Slip, John Jay, Carl Schurz, Hamilton Fish, St. Gabriel's, Corlears Hook, and John J. Murphy, the number of those playing at any one time was never more than 12.6 per cent of the total number of children living within a radius of one-quarter mile of the playground. All of the children attending Tompkins Square Playground on July 14, 1927, were requested to give their addresses and it was found that 725 of these children lived within a radius of one-quarter mile of the playground and only 255 beyond such a radius. This is the justification for regarding a quarter-mile radius as the area of effectiveness of a neighborhood playground. If, on the census taken of the nine playgrounds, not more than 12.6 per cent of the children of a neighborhood are found to play at any one time, it would seem to be an optimistic estimate that not more than 25 per cent of the children will want to play at any one time. This would seem to make due allowance for the fact that many children will not go to a playground because of the feeling that the space is inadequate or crowded. Of course this 25 per cent would not cover festival occasions or celebrations which would attract a larger number of the children.

Such evidence for the use of 300 square feet and one-fourth the total number of children may seem to be inadequate. However, they are only meant to be rough approximations. A change in either of these figures would not alter the results, in so far as the relative standings of the play districts are concerned. Making use of these standards, the amount of play space needed in a given play district can be computed by multiplying the total number of children by 300 and dividing by 4. In order to relate the play space in use in 1920 to the amount of space needed, it was necessary to discover in square feet how much play area was open in that year. These figures were secured from the Board of Education and the Park Department. They included park playgrounds, park athletic fields, public school playgrounds and athletic fields. The recreation piers were omitted from consideration because of the fact that they are used largely by adults and smaller children. The sum of these play spaces in each play district divided by the total number of square feet considered adequate, we shall call the index of play-space adequacy. This is expressed in terms of per cent as shown in the last column of Table 2 on the next page.

In computing these indices, several difficulties were experienced. The vacation school playgrounds were open only during the summer months, July and August. Of the 3304 arrests, 540 were made during these months. As this was found to be 16.33 per cent of the total, only one-sixth of the area of these school playgrounds was computed. Another difficulty was to include the play areas in Central Park. The radius of effectiveness of these areas is larger than that of neighborhood playgrounds. Whereas the census taken at Tompkins Square showed that 725 of the 980 children came from a radius of one-quarter mile, a similar census taken of the Heckscher playground in Central Park showed 1700 out of 2600 children coming from a radius of one mile. Thus,

TABLE 2. INDEX OF PLAY SPACE ADEQUACY BY DISTRICTS OF
MANHATTAN, 1920

Play District	Child Population	Play Space Needed (sq. ft.)	Play Space in Use—1920 (sq. ft.)	Adequacy Index—per cent
1	1,760	132,000	37,026	28.0
2	18,508	1,388,100	73,870	5.3
3	30,102	2,257,650	195,983	8.7
4	34,222	2,566,650	66,669	2.6
5	12,217	916,275	10,804	1.2
6	10,683	801,225	36,841	4.6
7	5,276	395,700	000	0.0
8	3,631	272,325	87,991	32.3
9	9,428	707,100	5,277	.7
10	9,740	730,500	61,504	8.4
11	6,377	478,275	2,275	.5
12	11,977	998,275	101,785	10.2
13	1,664	124,800	65,340	52.3
14	5,770	431,750	67,983	15.7
15	14,947	1,120,025	95,108	8.5
16	21,742	1,630,650	69,170	4.2
17	4,427	332,025	65,340	19.7
18	9,097	682,275	371,890	54.5
19	7,114	533,550	221,958	41.6
20	29,603	2,220,225	221,328	10.0
21	26,323	1,964,225	216,411	11.0
22	7,889	581,675	61,372	10.6
23	10,384	778,800	19,153	2.5
24	8,556	641,700	180,501	28.1
25	8,147	601,025	88,170	14.7
26	4,617	346,275	175,111	50.6
27	4,721	354,075	000	0.0
28	1,592	119,400	43,560	36.5

while this playground in the southern part of this park may be said to serve all of Manhattan, the immediate neighborhood does contribute the majority of the children.   In this case the area of the playground was divided among the three districts bordering the southern end of the park.   In the northern part of the park a somewhat different condition may be said to exist.   There, there are 30 acres of playing fields which draw from the entire island and for which permits to play group games are granted to children from all sections. However, the Park Department estimated that about 50 per cent of the drawing power of those athletic fields was in the immediate neighborhood, so that one-half of this area was divided among the three play districts adjoining the northern end of the park.   The influence of Van Cortlandt Park was left out of consideration entirely and we shall see its probable effect on the play districts in the northern end of Manhattan.

On two outline maps of Manhattan, these indices, delinquency and play-space adequacy, were then charted.   For purposes of comparison the cross-hatching was done so as to be able to note their similarity or dissimilarity at a glance. On the first chart, the four districts having the heaviest shading represent the districts of highest proportionate delinquency while on the second map, the same shading represents the four having the smallest adequacy indices.   On the basis of a superficial comparison of the maps, there seems to be a certain amount of association between the two factors.   Five of the 28 districts show exactly similar shading, while 15 others show shadings separated by only one degree.   On the other hand, some show a wide divergence.   Even though play district 1 shows a high adequacy index, it has also a high delinquency index.   District 8 reveals the same situation, whereas district 16 has a relatively low amount of play space but also a low proportion of delinquency.   The situation in district 27 is the same as that in 16.

PROPORTION OF JUVENILE DELINQUENTS
TO CHILD POPULATION (7-15 YRS.)
OF MANHATTAN BY DISTRICTS (1920)

PLAY SPACE ADEQUACY OF MAN-
HATTAN BY DISTRICTS (1920)

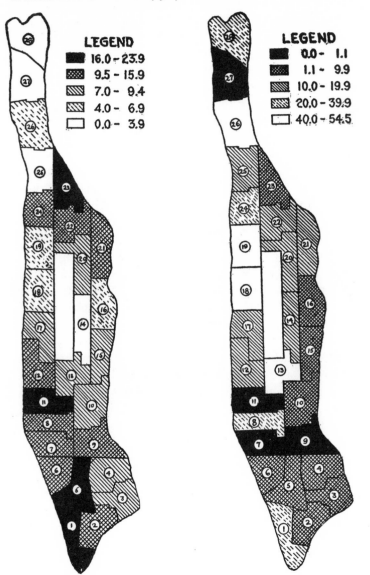

LEGEND

16.0 – 23.9
9.5 – 15.9
7.0 – 9.4
4.0 – 6.9
0.0 – 3.9

LEGEND

0.0 – 1.1
1.1 – 9.9
10.0 – 19.9
20.0 – 39.9
40.0 – 54.5

The degree of resemblance between these two factors represented in these charts was reduced to a mathematical expression by means of a rank correlation. This computation with the method employed and the resulting coefficient will be found in Table A, Appendix E. Owing to the small number of cases, a coefficient of correlation of + .44 is to be viewed with some caution. The probable error is high and this likewise is due to the small number of cases. However, it is to be noted that this coefficient, + .44 is probably the lowest that we could get. For example, district 27 is located in the northern part of the island, has a relatively scattered population and consequently a large amount of open space for recreation. It is flanked on both sides by parks, Fort Washington Park to the west and Highbridge Park to the east, and is not far from Van Cortlandt Park. But because of the fact that there was no supervised play area in use in this region in 1920, its index of play-space adequacy was 0.0. There was no way of assigning to this and to similar regions its ranking in respect to nearness to parks and consequently the results are liable to err on the side unfavorable to the association. If this play district had an adequacy index comparable to that of the district just to the north of it, the coefficient of correlation would be raised as much as .10. Granting that the mathematical measure of association here reached is probably a low one, taking into account other known facts about each of the play districts, it is a mark of moderate, if not highly significant, association.

We are not on safe ground, however, if we stop here. Unless some of the other environmental factors which are usually regarded as contributing to the production of delinquency are taken account of, we fall into the same mistakes of which we accused the investigations mentioned in the last chapter. Let us see, then, whether by checking the con-

clusion to which we have just arrived by the examination of
other factors we can either disprove or confirm the hypothesis
of the association between play areas and juvenile delinquency.

One of the factors most frequently mentioned as a contributing cause to the making of a delinquent is that of
population congestion. The statement is often made that
the greatest number of arrests for delinquency comes from
the crowded sections of the cities. It would be a strange
thing indeed if the most densely populated portions of a city
did not furnish the majority of the delinquents. But merely
to say that the neighborhoods with the densest populations
provide the greatest amount of delinquency and reason from
that to congestion as a contributing factor in the making of
crime, is all wrong. The more important question to ask is
whether or not these crowded areas supply the highest proportionate amount of juvenile delinquents. Is it true that in
Manhattan the highest indices of delinquency are in the
sections having the highest percentage of population per acre?

In order to answer this question a third chart was made
similar to the two mentioned above. Using the same play
districts as units, the area of each was computed in acres
and then by dividing the child population of the district by
the number of acres, a figure was reached which represented
the child density per acre. The 28 districts were then
ranked, beginning with the highest density per acre as rank 1.
The accompanying map shows the results of this study, the
four districts shaded most heavily representing the four with
the highest density, the next nine districts those having a
smaller density index, and so on. The cross-hatching was
done in this fashion so as to make the map comparable with
the previous map on delinquency.

There does not seem to be as much agreement between the
delinquency and the density maps as between the adequacy

CHILDREN (7-15 YRS.) PER ACRE IN MANHATTAN BY DISTRICTS (1920)

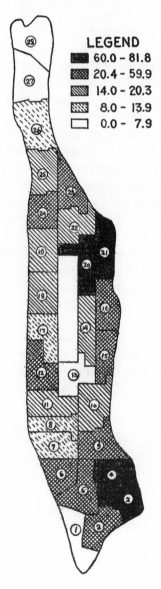

and delinquency maps. While it is true that the shadings of districts 5, 6, 10, 12, 24, 26, 27, 28 are similar, it is also true that there is a wide diversity in such districts as 1, 4, 7, 11, 16, and 20. To reduce this graphic presentation to a mathematical statement, the method of rank correlation was used similar to that used in comparing the two former indices, with results as shown in Table B, Appendix E.

On the basis of a coefficient of correlation of $+ .21$ with a probable error of .18, it is very doubtful if there is any significant association in Manhattan between the factors of child density per acre and the proportion of juvenile delinquency. However, it may be unjust to dismiss this factor from consideration, on the ground that the small number of cases considered is not large enough to reach a final statement. While the size of the coefficient does not warrant its inclusion, let us assume that there is some connection between the factor of child density and delinquency and take it into account in making the comparisons which are to follow.

Another factor which is usually given a large place among the contributing causes to juvenile delinquency is that of the racial composition of the population. Early reports of the study being carried on by the Illinois Institute of Juvenile Research, mentioned above,[1] seemed to indicate that as the character of a neighborhood changed as to racial composition, the amount of delinquency coming from that neighborhood changed also. One of the first questions that juvenile court officers ask when a child is brought before them is, from what section of the city does he come, a neighborhood that is predominantly Italian, Russian, Jewish, Irish, Austrian, or some other. It may fairly be said that there is a general consensus of opinion which ascribes to the conflict of cultures which one finds in the foreign sectors of our large cities a prominent rôle in the production of juvenile delinquency.

[1] *Ibid.*, p. 132.

Let us see, then, whether nationality groupings in Manhattan appear to be a dominant factor in the amount of delinquency.   Taking again the figures for 1920, which nationalities contributed the largest proportions to the delinquency totals?   In examining the data, it was found that in some cases the parents were foreign-born and the children native-born.   In such instances, where either the child or the parent was foreign-born, the case was counted as that of a foreign-born.   The data grouped themselves as shown in Table 3.

TABLE 3. CONTRIBUTIONS BY NATIONALITIES TO DELINQUENCY
TOTALS FOR 1920

Nationality	Number of Cases	Percentage of Total
Italian...........................	1016	30.75
Russian	564	17.1
Irish	234	7.1
Negroes and Colored	183	5.5
Austrian	177	5.4
Polish	71	2.1
Hungarian	48	1.5
United States.	684	20.7
Scattered......................	327	9.9

The Italians lead all other nationalities in the number of cases which they as a group contribute to the court.   However, it cannot be inferred from this that the Italian children or children of Italian parents are racially more delinquent than the other nationalities mentioned.   To discover this fact, it is necessary to inquire whether this group supplies more delinquents in proportion to their total numbers in the entire population of Manhattan.   By relating the above figures to the totals for each of the racial groups living in the island, it was found that the Italians contributed 2.84 cases per thousand of Italian population; the native-born of native parentage, 1.76; the Russians, 1.60; the negroes and colored, 1.58; the Polish, 1.10; the Austrian, 1.07; the Irish .79 and the Hungarian .68.

Here, then, we have three environmental factors which are supposed to be related to the production of delinquency, i.e., child density per acre, racial composition of the population and the presence or absence of play areas. Now there are certain sanitary districts in Manhattan which are accessible to play spaces and other areas which are relatively inaccessible. By this is meant that some have, either within or on their borders, playgrounds which are of easy access to all the children in that district, while in others, it would be necessary for the children to travel as far as three-quarters of a mile to a play space. If sanitary districts could be found which are contiguous and which have about the same density per acre and racial characteristics, but differ only in their nearness to play areas it might be possible to discover the effectiveness of such areas. The problem here is simply that of holding constant the two factors, child density and nationality status, while a comparison is made of the influence of the presence or absence of a playground on the amount of delinquency. It is obvious, of course, that those districts must be selected in which there is a large amount of delinquency so as to eliminate the aleatory element. Contiguous areas were chosen in order that the other environmental factors, such as, economic condition of the people, presence of industries, etc., might be said to remain fairly constant.

Twelve such comparisons were made. The sanitary districts had to be selected from the sections which contributed the most cases to the court, viz., the lower East Side, the lower West Side, the upper West Side, the upper East Side and the Harlem District. More cases would have been chosen but for the obvious difficulty of getting contiguous areas, differing as to access to a playground, but similar as to child density per acre and racial composition. In each of the comparisons made it was necessary to compute the child density per acre, the ratio between the foreign-born and the total population of the district, and an index of delinquency which was reached by dividing the number of arrests by the child population, 7 to 15 years old, of the sanitary district.

SANITARY DISTRICT 4

Boundaries — Clinton, Scammel, Division Streets and the East River
Child Density per acre — 82.4
Racial Composition — 46.5 per cent Russian; 1.4 per cent Austrian; .5 per cent Italian
Delinquency Index — 9.0 per thousand

SANITARY DISTRICT 6

Boundaries — Pike, Clinton, Division Streets and the East River
Child Density per acre — 83.4
Racial Composition — 49 per cent Russian; 1.2 per cent Austrian; 3.3 per cent Italian
Delinquency Index — 9.5 per thousand

These sanitary areas are on the lower East Side. Both may be said to be equally accessible to playgrounds. The child density is about the same. The very slight difference in the percentage of delinquency may be accounted for on the basis of the slight difference in racial composition, both districts being predominantly Russian with the latter having a slightly higher per cent than the former.

SANITARY DISTRICT 10

Boundaries — Grand, Rivington, Cannon Streets and the East River
Child Density per acre — 68.2
Racial Composition — 13.6 per cent Austrian; 12.5 per cent Italian; 12.2 per cent Russian; 7.0 per cent Polish
Delinquency Index — 14.3 per thousand

SANITARY DISTRICT 16

Boundaries — Old Bowery, Norfolk, Division and Grand Streets
Child Density per acre — 56.0
Racial Composition — 26 per cent Russian; 10.6 per cent Italian;
9.8 per cent Polish; 2.6 per cent Austrian
Delinquency Index — 11.2 per thousand

These districts are on the lower East Side. The former may be said to be relatively inaccessible to a play area while the latter is accessible. It is true that the latter has a smaller density but considering the fact that the latter has a much higher proportion of Russians who next to the Italians contribute the highest proportion of cases to the court, it is significant that this district has a lower delinquency index. The influence of the play space would seem to be marked in this instance.

SANITARY DISTRICT 26

Boundaries — Avenue B, Avenue D, between East Third and East Ninth Streets
Child Density per acre — 123.4
Racial Composition — 22.1 per cent Russian; 15.4 Polish; 11.6 per cent Austrian
Delinquency Index — 5.6 per thousand

SANITARY DISTRICT 30

Boundaries — Allen, Clinton, Rivington and East Third Streets
Child Density per acre — 107.7
Racial Composition — 21.2 per cent Russian; 14.5 per cent Polish; 12.4 per cent Austrian
Delinquency Index — 12.4 per thousand

The comparison in this case is very striking. District 26 is easily accessible to a play area while district 30 is inaccessible. The racial composition is very similar and the child density factor is in favor of the latter. Despite this fact, the district which is accessible shows a delinquency index of less than one-half of that of the inaccessible district.

SANITARY DISTRICT 34

Boundaries — East Ninth Street to East Fourteenth Street between First Avenue and Avenue B
Child Density per acre — 92.1
Racial Composition — 29.3 per cent Italian; 11.3 per cent Russian; 8.9 per cent Polish; 2.2 per cent Austrian
Delinquency Index — 12.4 per thousand

SANITARY DISTRICT 40

Boundaries — East Fourteenth Street to East Nineteenth Street, between Third Avenue and First Avenue
Child Density per acre — 67.5
Racial Composition — 21.9 per cent Italian; 16.2 per cent Russian; 5.4 per cent Polish; 4.7 per cent Austrian
Delinquency Index — 14.2 per thousand

Of these two districts, 34 is accessible to a play area while 40 is inaccessible. One would expect that considering the child density per acre and the difference in proportion of Italians which more than makes up for the difference in Russians, the former would show a higher delinquency index than the latter. But since the reverse is true, some significance must be attached to the influence of the play space.

SANITARY DISTRICT 18

Boundaries — Grand, Rivington, Norfolk Streets and Bowery
Child Density per acre — 93.7
Racial Composition — 28.1 per cent Russian; 8.2 per cent Italian; 6.1 per cent Austrian; 4.3 per cent Polish
Delinquency Index — 10.7 per thousand

SANITARY DISTRICT 28

Boundaries — East Ninth Street to East Fourteenth Street, between Avenues B and D
Child Density per acre — 83.0
Racial Composition — 23.2 per cent Russian; 16.8 per cent Polish; 5.0 per cent Austrian; 3.8 per cent Italian
Delinquency Index — 7.9 per thousand

Here, the districts are similar as to child density. The former contains a higher proportion of Italians and Russians but this might be considered to be offset by the much greater proportion of Poles in the latter. No. 18 is not accessible to a playground while No. 28 is. However, the difference in the amount of delinquency here might not be associated with the presence of a play space inasmuch as the areas are not so contiguous and therefore not so comparable.

SANITARY DISTRICT 32

Boundaries — East Third Street to East Ninth Street, between First Avenue and Avenue B
Child Density per acre — 57.5
Racial Composition — 21.0 per cent Russian; 15.5 per cent Polish; 7.3 per cent Austrian; 3.1 per cent Italian
Delinquency Index — 5.7 per thousand

SANITARY DISTRICT 38

Boundaries — East Third Street to East Ninth Street, between Third Avenue and First Avenue
Child Density per acre — 71.2
Racial Composition — 20.3 per cent Russian; 11.2 per cent Polish; 8.6 per cent Italian; 6.5 per cent Austrian
Delinquency Index — 4.6 per thousand

These two districts are similar in racial composition and fairly similar as to child density per acre. Part of Tompkins Square is located in the former. The delinquency index in 32 is higher than that in 38 which is contrary to what we would expect on the basis of the hypothesis with which these comparisons were begun.

SANITARY DISTRICT 29

Boundaries — Canal, Pearl, Centre Streets and Bowery-Park Row
Child Density per acre — 66.5

Racial Composition — 32.0 per cent Italian
Delinquency Index — 11.7 per thousand

SANITARY DISTRICT 43

Boundaries — Spring Street to East Houston Street, between
    Broadway and Bowery
Child Density per acre — 70.5
Racial Composition — 40.7 per cent Italian
Delinquency Index — 18.3 per thousand

Sanitary Districts 29 and 43 are on the lower West Side.
They are predominantly Italian. The former is accessible
to a play area; the latter is not. It is true that the latter has
a greater proportion of Italians and this may give rise to the
difference in the amount of delinquency although it would
seem as though the indices were too widely separated to be
accounted for on this ground.

SANITARY DISTRICT 47

Boundaries — Spring, Wooster, Broome, Broadway, Canal,
    Sullivan and Macdougal Streets
Child Density per acre — 30.5
Racial Composition — 38.6 per cent Italian
Delinquency Index — 17.3 per thousand

SANITARY DISTRICT 49

Boundaries — West Houston, Broadway, Broome, Wooster,
    Spring and Macdougal Streets
Child Density per acre — 41.8
Racial Composition — 47.4 per cent Italian
Delinquency Index — 23.0 per thousand

SANITARY DISTRICT 67

Boundaries — Barrow, West Fourth, Hancock, West Houston
    and Hudson Streets
Child Density per acre — 63.3
Racial Composition — 39.0 per cent Italian
Delinquency Index — 12.6 per thousand

In this case, three districts on the lower West Side were compared. The two former are relatively inaccessible, the latter relatively accessible, to playgrounds. While the difference between 47 and 49 might very well be accounted for, in respect to their delinquencies, by the difference in the proportion of Italians, the same cannot be said with regard to a comparison between 47 and 67. In these two, the proportions of Italians are about the same, the child density is very much in favor of the former, and yet the latter shows a lower deliquency index. Either other factors of more importance are operative or else we have to conclude that the playground has some influence on the amount of delinquency.

SANITARY DISTRICT 123

Boundaries — West Forty Second Street to West Forty Sixth Street, between Tenth Avenue and the Hudson River
Child Density per acre — 23.6
Racial Composition — 6.7 per cent Irish; 4.0 per cent Austrian; 3.1 per cent Italian; 1.5 per cent Polish; 1.3 per cent Russian
Delinquency Index — 16.6 per thousand

SANITARY DISTRICT 129

Boundaries — West Forty Sixth Street to West Fiftieth Street, between Tenth Avenue and Hudson River
Child Density per acre — 31.4
Racial Composition — 9.9 per cent Irish; 2.4 per cent Polish; 1.9 per cent Russian; 1.3 per cent Italian; .7 per cent Austrian
Delinquency Index — 15.3 per thousand

Districts 123 and 129 are on the upper West Side. The former is relatively inaccessible to a playground while the latter is relatively accessible. However, the differences in child density per acre and in racial composition together with the fact that there were only a small number of arrests in each, 20 in the former and 25 in the latter, make any comparisons of somewhat doubtful value.

SANITARY DISTRICT 156

Boundaries — East Ninety Fourth Street to East Ninety Ninth
    Street, between Third Avenue and First Avenue
Child Density per acre — 83.0
Racial Composition — 15.7 per cent Russian; 6.5 per cent
    Italian; 6.0 per cent Irish; 3.6 per cent Austrian
Delinquency Index — 9.8 per thousand

SANITARY DISTRICT 164

Boundaries — East Ninety Ninth Street to East One Hundred and Fourth Street, between Third Avenue and First
    Avenue
Child Density per acre — 127.7
Racial Composition — 23.3 per cent Russian; 11.2 per cent
    Italian; 4.0 per cent Austrian; 1.2 per cent Irish
Delinquency Index — 9.5 per thousand

In these two districts, the comparison should favor the former. They are located on the upper East Side. The former, being accessible, has a lower child density and also fewer Russians and Italians, those nationalities which contribute the largest numbers to the court. Yet this district has a slightly higher delinquency index than the latter which is relatively inaccessible. This is contrary to what might be expected on the hypothesis of the play area as a factor in the prevention of delinquency.

SANITARY DISTRICT 172

Boundaries — East One Hundred and Fifth Street to East One
    Hundred and Twelfth Street, between Park Avenue and
    Third Avenue
Child Density per acre — 66.8
Racial Composition — 18.8 per cent Russian; 10.0 per cent
    Italian; 5.0 per cent Irish; 2.6 per cent Austrian
Delinquency Index — 9.1 per thousand

SANITARY DISTRICT 182

Boundaries — East One Hundred and Twelfth Street to East
  One Hundred and Nineteenth Street, between Park
  Avenue and Third Avenue
Child Density per acre — 61.0
Racial Composition — 21.2 per cent Russian; 8.6 per cent
  Italian; 5.1 per cent Austrian; 3.4 per cent Irish
Delinquency Index — 9.9 per thousand

Here are two districts also on the upper East Side. They
are about equally accessible to play areas. They are very
similar as to child density and racial composition and they
show striking similarity in their indices of delinquency.

SANITARY DISTRICT 212

Boundaries — West One Hundred Thirty Third Street and
  West One Hundred and Fortieth Street, between Fifth
  Avenue and Lenox Avenue
Child Density per acre — 30.3
Racial Composition — 96.3 Negroes and Mulattoes
Delinquency Index — 36.1 per thousand

SANITARY DISTRICT 230

Boundaries — West One Hundred Thirty Eighth Street and
  West One Hundred and Forty Second Street, between
  Eighth Avenue and Lenox Avenue
Child Density per acre — 30.9
Racial Composition — 88.5 per cent Negroes and Mulattoes
Delinquency Index — 25.6 per thousand

SANITARY DISTRICT 232

Boundaries — West One Hundred and Forty Second Street
  and West One Hundred and Forty Sixth Street, between
  Eighth Avenue and Lenox Avenue
Child Density per acre — 43.0
Racial Composition — 65.1 per cent Negroes and Mulattoes
Delinquency Index — 20.0 per thousand

The comparison of these three districts in the Harlem section is very interesting. They are all equally inaccessible to play areas. They are similar as to child density per acre. It is rather significant that the delinquency indices vary according to the differences in the racial composition of the areas. In this case, the factors of child density and play areas may be said to be constant with a variation in the racial characteristics of the population. This would seem to be evidence for regarding the racial factor as a contributing factor to the amount of delinquency.

While the evidence offered by these comparisons is far from conclusive by itself, it does serve to corroborate the conclusions drawn from relating the index of delinquency with that of play-space adequacy. In only two of the district comparisons were the results quite the reverse of what was to have been expected on the basis of the hypothesis that the presence of play areas does have some influence on delinquency. These comparisons likewise serve to substantiate the previous assertion, namely, that when we attempt to discover the contributing environmental factors in the making of a delinquent, we are not long in discovering that the problem is a highly complicated one. The present study is in the nature of an exploratory analysis endeavoring to set forth a method of evaluating the effect of some of the possible environmental influences.

Another question that might be raised has to do with the matter of " lag " in the problem of juvenile delinquency. The mean age of the children with whom this study has to do was 12.8 years. It is justifiable to raise the question of whether or not the delinquent child is a product of a lack of facilities for recreation years ago. A child who at 13 commits an offense did it probably because his early home or other conditioning was defective. In other words, the environmental factors contributing most heavily to the delinquent in 1920 might very well have been environmental factors which were inadequate in 1910 or 1912. The only answer that we can give to this is to say that there has not been a significant change in the play areas available in crowded Manhattan in the past ten or fifteen years. There doubtless has been a great improvement in the supervision provided. It is rather difficult to deny that if there had been more adequate supervision of children's play in Manhattan in 1915 there would have been less delinquency in 1920. The fundamental assumption underlying the parole system as applied to youthful offenders is that with the proper direction of their activities their criminalistic tendencies can be corrected.

A query which has considerable bearing on the above analysis is that of the character of police regulation and control. In the districts which have been considered, is the vigilance of the police fairly uniform as between various sections of the city? This is significant for the reason that if a child in one of the play districts is more liable to be arraigned before the court for a minor offense than a child in another region, then any conclusions regarding the significance of play areas are invalidated. If a child on the lower East Side breaks a window in playing ball on the street, is it likely that the police will overlook the offense in view of the more serious crimes committed in that neighborhood than would be the case in the northern part of the island? In view of the fact that the cases are reviewed before a child is arraigned, it would seem to be true that the police jurisdiction might be regarded as more or less uniform.

A method for checking this last statement was devised by a simple process of grouping the various offenses into categories of more serious and less serious. All of the offenses were first catalogued and then with the aid of the officials of the court these were divided into the two classes as follows :

More Serious	*Less Serious*
Burglary	Begging
Carrying Dangerous Weapons	Crime Against Nature
Discharging Fire-Arms	Disorderly Child
Disorderly Conduct (Aggravated)	Disorderly Conduct (Conscious Act)
False Alarm of Fire	
Felonious Assault	Disorderly Conduct (Simple)
Forgery	Injury to Property
Grand Larceny	Peddling
Having Burglar's Instruments	Petit Larceny
Having Narcotics in Possession	Simple Assault
Material Witness (Fornication)	Ungovernable Child
Rape	Violation of the Corporation Ordinance
Robbery	
Unlawful Entry	

The purpose in making this classification was to determine whether the proportion that the two categories bear to each other varies greatly from play district to play district. For the island as a whole, 1391 of the 3304 cases, or 42.1 per cent were more serious, while 1913, or 57.9 belonged to the less serious group. If the 28 play districts show in each of them these same relative proportions, it would be fair to say that the matter of police regulation is uniform throughout Manhattan. It is interesting to note from Table 4 on the next page, that in twenty-three of the twenty-eight play districts the relative proportions are approximately the same as the relative proportions that the totals in the two categories bear to each other. In only five of the districts are the proportions decidedly reversed. Apart from any other considerations, the fact that before a child is arraigned before the children's court, he is turned over to the Society for the Prevention of Cruelty to Children, would serve to insure a reasonable amount of uniformity in the character of offenses for which children reach the court. Such a clearing-house for cases would prevent a very wide variation in the character of police regulation.

TABLE 4. RELATIONS BETWEEN TOTAL ARRESTS FOR MORE SERIOUS
AND LESS SERIOUS OFFENSES

Play District	Total Arrests	More Serious	More Serious (Per cent)	Less Serious (Per cent)
I	42	24	57.1	42.9
2	232	117	50.4	49.6
3	281	121	43.1	56.9
4	301	125	41.5	58.5
5	211	102	48.3	51.7
6	148	65	43.9	56.1
7	73	30	41.1	58.9
8	42	20	47.6	52.4
9	126	45	35.7	64.3
10	87	31	35.6	64.4
11	117	77	65.8	34.2
12	181	85	47.0	53.0
13	13	7	53.8	46.2
14	19	4	28.6	71.4
15	116	43	37.1	62.9
16	128	46	35.9	64.1
17	41	20	48.8	51.2
18	58	18	31.0	69.0
19	37	18	48.6	51.4
20	234	71	30.3	69.7
21	346	126	36.4	63.6
22	102	36	35.3	64.7
23	201	79	39.3	60.7
24	81	37	45.7	54.3
25	30	14	47.0	53.0
26	32	15	46.9	53.1
27	19	14	73.7	26.3
28	6	2	33.3	66.6
Entire Island....	3304	1391	42.1	57.9

On the whole, then, what variation does exist in police regulation from one district to another is not sufficient to invalidate the conclusions of the previous part of this study. It goes without saying that the children who committed the more serious offenses are those who will form the majority of those who become adult criminals. The *a priori* assumption is perhaps justified that in this class would be found the greatest number of those who are mentally defective and certainly more difficult to reach by supervised play than the latter group of less serious offenders. The right amount of adequately supervised playing space might be said to be more effective with the group whose offenses come under the classification of less serious. Eleven of the twenty-three districts mentioned above show a higher proportion of less serious offenses than would be expected. It would be interesting to know how many of these districts show a play-space adequacy below the mean for that of the island. These eleven districts are numbers 9, 10, 14, 15, 16, 18, 20, 21, 22, 23, 28. Of these, nine: 9, 10, 14, 15, 16, 20, 21, 22, and 23 have a play space adequacy lower than that of the mean for the entire twenty-eight districts. Might this indicate that a higher amount of play space per child would diminish the proportion of petty offenses committed in these neighborhoods?

SUMMARY

In the Introduction to this study, we set ourselves two questions. The first of these was " How did we get this way? " and the second, " What are we going to do about it? " In Part One we endeavored to answer the first of these queries in the matter of legislation for public recreation. We there summarized the main features of that legislation for the past twelve years. Part Two has been concerned with the second question, namely, " What are we going to do about it? " The state has gone into the field of making provision for recreation on the basis of the police power, which carries the implication that such legislation is for the general welfare of society. It may be true that the provision of recreational opportunities is promoting the common good but very little in the way of objective evidence is at hand to demonstrate that it does any such thing.

One of the claims in behalf of recreation is that the provision of recreation spaces will reduce juvenile delinquency. In an effort to answer the question of whether or not there is any association between play areas and delinquency, this analysis was pursued. By way of introduction, the various methods by which the problem has been attacked were considered and criticized. Manhattan Island was chosen for investigation and the year studied was 1920. By relating the amount of delinquency coming from certain defined districts to the inadequacy of play space in those districts, a measure of association was found between these two factors which expressed in mathematical terms was a correlation coefficient of $+ .44$. To check this result by means of other environmental factors which are generally supposed to contribute to the production of delinquency, the factors of child density and racial composition were held constant in relating pairs of sanitary districts which differed in accessibility to play spaces. As a final check, the question of the uniformity of police regulation among the play districts of the island was considered.

From the evidence gathered, we can say that a certain amount of association between recreation areas and juvenile delinquency appears to exist. This is quite a different statement, however, from one which would assign to the presence of recreation spaces the controlling factor in the prevention of delinquency. On the basis of this scientific exploration, we should have arrived at two very definite conclusions. In the first place, we should look with considerable skepticism on any easy generalization which would assign to this one environmental factor, viz., recreation spaces, the predominating influence in the control of delinquency.   In the second place, we should be able to say that there appears to be a moderate association between the presence of recreation areas and the absence of juvenile delinquency, provided we have taken into account a sufficient number of the environmental influences.

APPENDIX A

State Laws and Local Ordinances Covering the Main Features of a Recreation System

As set forth in the body of the text (p. 56) there are no norms by which to judge of the adequacy of legislation in a given state granting to municipalities and local governmental units powers concerning public recreation. The Playground and Recreation Association of America has been active in the fostering of state legislation, and while that organization has despaired of drafting a model law which will suit all conditions, it has made suggestions to state legislatures concerning the main features of such a model law. The conclusions of this organization with regard to the provisions which the state laws should contain have grown out of the experiences and difficulties which localities have met in the institution of a program of public recreation. For this reason, a copy of a law suggested by the Playground and Recreation Association is included here.

Suggested Draft of Bill for Enactment by Legislatures

An Act Empowering Municipalities to Provide, Maintain and Conduct a Supervised Recreation System and to Acquire, Establish, Conduct and Maintain Playgrounds, Athletic Fields, Gymnasiums, Public Baths, Swimming Pools, and Indoor Recreation Centers; and Authorising School Districts to Join in the Acquisition, Establishment, Conduct and Maintenance of Such Systems and Facilities.

Section 1. This act shall apply to cities of the second and third class, to counties, towns (townships), and villages (boroughs).

The term "municipality" as used in this act includes only a city of the second or third class or any county, town (township), or village (borough).

Section 2. The city council or *governing body* of any city of the second or third class or the county commissioners or governing body of any county or the town council or governing body of any town (township), or the board of trustees or governing body of any village (borough) may dedicate and set apart for use as playgrounds, athletic fields, gymnasiums, public baths, swimming pools and indoor recreation centers, or any one or more of these, any lands or buildings, or both, owned or leased by such municipality and not dedicated or devoted to another and inconsistent public use; and such municipality may, in such manner as may now or hereafter be authorised or provided by law for the acquisition of lands or buildings for public purposes in such municipality, acquire or lease lands or buildings, or both (in such municipality) for the playgrounds, athletic fields, gymnasiums, public baths, swimming pools, indoor recreation centers or any one or more of these purposes; or if there be no law authorising such acquisition or leasing of such lands or buildings, the governing body of any such municipality is hereby empowered to acquire lands or buildings, or both, for such purposes by gift, purchase, condemnation or lease.

Section 3. The city council or governing body of any city of the second or third class or the county commissioners or governing body of any county or the town council or governing body of any town (township) or the board of trustees or governing body of any village (borough) shall have the power to provide, establish, maintain and conduct a system of supervised recreation which shall include any one or more of the following activities and facilities, viz, playgrounds, athletic fields, gymnasiums, public baths, swimming pools and indoor recreation centers; and the authority to provide, establish, maintain and conduct such supervised recreation system and facilities may be vested by the said governing body in the school board, park board or recreation commission as the governing body of such municipality, county, town (township), village (borough) may determine. Any such board, body or commission in which shall be vested by appropriate action of the said governing body the right to provide, establish, maintain and conduct such recreation system and facilities, shall have the power to equip such playgrounds, athletic fields, gymnasiums, public baths, swimming pools and indoor recreation centers and the buildings thereon, and may for the purpose of carrying out the provision of this act employ play leaders, playground directors, supervisors, recreation superintendents or such other officers or employees as they deem proper.

Section 4. If the governing body of any such city, county, town (township) or village (borough) shall determine that the power to provide, establish, conduct and maintain a supervised recreation system, including playgrounds, athletic fields, gymnasiums, public baths, swimming pools and indoor recreation centers or any one or more of these, and to acquire by gift, purchase, eminent domain or lease, lands and buildings for such purposes, shall be exercised by a recreation board or commission, the school board or park board such governing body shall by resolution or ordinance vest such powers in such body and the body to which such powers and duties shall be thus delegated shall have the same powers which the said governing body would have had to effectually carry out the purposes of this act. Provided, however, that if there is not a recreation board or commission in existence and it is the desire of the governing body to vest the said powers, duties and responsibilities in a recreation board or commission, then the said governing body shall have the power to create such board or commission, which shall consist of five persons, two of whom shall be members of the school board to be appointed by the mayor or presiding officer of such governing body, to serve for terms of five years or until their successors are appointed, except that the members of such board or commission first appointed shall be appointed for such terms that the term of one member shall expire annually thereafter. The members of such board or commission shall serve without pay. Vacancies in such board or commission occurring

otherwise than by expiration of term shall be filled only for
the unexpired term and such appointment shall be filled by the
mayor or presiding officer of the governing body.

Section 5. Any two or more municipalities may jointly provide, establish, maintain and conduct a supervised recreation
system and acquire property for and establish and maintain
playgrounds, athletic fields, gymnasiums, public baths, swimming pools and indoor recreation centers or any one or more of
these. The school board or district shall have the power to
join with any municipality or municipalities in providing, establishing, conducting and maintaining such supervised recreation
system and facilities.

Section 6. A recreation board or commission or other authority in which is vested the power to provide, establish, maintain
and conduct a supervised recreation system including playgrounds, athletic fields, gymnasiums, public baths, swimming
pools, and indoor recreation centers, or any or more of these,
pursuant to this act may accept any grant or devise of real estate
or any gift or bequest of money or other personal property or
any donation to be applied principal or income for either temporary or permanent use for playgrounds or recreation purposes, but if the acceptance thereof for such purpose will subject the municipality to additional expense for improvement,
maintenance, or renewal, the acceptance of any grant or devise
of real estate shall be subject to the approval of the governing
body of such municipality. Money received for such purpose
unless otherwise provided by the terms of the gift or bequest
shall be deposited with the treasurer of the municipality to the
account of the recreation board or commission or other body
having charge of such work and the same may be withdrawn and
paid out in the same manner as money appropriated for recreation purposes.

Section 7. The governing body of any municipality may provide that the bonds of such municipality may be deemed in the
manner provided by law for the issuance of bonds for other
purposes, for the purpose of acquiring lands or buildings for
playgrounds, athletic fields, gymnasiums, public baths, swim-

ming pools or indoor recreation centers, or any one or more of them, and for the equipment thereof subject however to the adoption of a proposition thereof at a municipal election if the adoption of such a proposition is a prerequisite to the issuance of bonds of such municipality for public purposes generally.

Section 8. Whenever a petition signed by at least two per cent of the qualified and registered voters in any municipality shall be filed in the office of the clerk of such municipality, requesting the governing body of such municipality to provide, establish, maintain and conduct a supervised recreation system and to levy an annual tax for the conduct and maintenance thereof of not less than . . . mills nor more than . . . mills on each dollar of assessed valuation of all taxable property within the corporate limits of such municipality, it shall be the duty of the governing body of such municipality to cause the question of the establishment, maintenance and conduct of such supervised recreation system, including playgrounds, athletic fields, gymnasiums, public baths, swimming pools and indoor recreation centers, or such of them as in the judgment of the governing body it may be advisable and practicable to provide, conduct and maintain out of the tax funds thus provided, to be submitted to the voters to be voted upon at the next general or special municipal election, provided however that such question shall not be voted upon at the next general or special election unless such petition shall have been filed at least thirty days prior to the date of such election.

Section 9. Upon the adoption of such proposition at such election this governing body of the municipality shall by appropriate resolution provide for the establishment, maintenance and conduct of such supervised recreation system, including playgrounds, athletic fields, gymnasiums, public baths, swimming pools and indoor recreation centers, or such one or more of these as they may deem advisable and practicable to be provided and maintained out of the tax money thus voted. And the said governing body may designate, by appropriate resolution or ordinance the body or commission to be vested with the powers, duties and obligations necessary for the establishment, maintenance and conduct of such recreation system, as provided in Section 3 of this act.

Section 10. The governing body of any municipality adopting the provisions of this act at an election shall thereafter annually levy and collect a tax of not less than the minimum nor more than the maximum amount set out in the said petition for such election, which tax shall be designated as the " playground and recreation tax " and shall be levied and collected in like manner as the general tax of the municipality, but the same shall be in addition to and exclusive of all other taxes such municipality may levy or collect, nor shall such tax be scaled down under any existing law.

Section 11. All expenses incurred under this act for the establishment, maintenance and conduct of a supervised recreation system of playgrounds, athletic fields, gymnasiums, public baths, swimming pools and indoor recreation centers, or any one or more of these, shall be paid from taxes provided for in Section 10 of this act.

Section 12. This act shall take effect immediately (upon publication of the statutes).

The main provisions of this law group themselves under these heads:

1. *Governmental Units Affected* — This embraces all the local units of government within a state: cities, towns, villages, boroughs, counties, townships.

2. *How Lands and Buildings to be Used for Recreation are to be Obtained* — This includes the use of lands and buildings already owned or leased by the municipality, the acquisition by law of other lands, or if there be no law, the power to acquire such lands by gift, purchase, condemnation, or lease.

3. *Authority Vested In* — School Board, Park Board, or Recreation Commission.

4. *Recreation Facilities Over Which the Powers Granted Extend* — Playgrounds, athletic fields, gymnasiums, public baths, swimming pools, and indoor recreation centers.

5. *Organization, Powers and Duties of the Recreation Commission* — This includes the manner of appointment, the term of office, the filling of vacancies, and the provision that two members of the school board shall be members of this commission.

6. *Joint Conduct* — by two or more local political units or by a combination of the school board and a governmental body.

7. *Institution of a Program of Public Recreation* — shall be made possible by a petition signed by at least two per cent of the qualified voters, followed by a popular referendum on the subject. This popular referendum shall include the maximum amount of tax which the municipality may levy.

8. *Tax Levied for Recreation to be in Addition to the Taxable Limit of the Municipality.*

The following summary digest of the provisions of the laws in the twenty-one states which have passed home-rule enabling acts will reveal the extent to which such laws follow this suggested act or deviate widely from it.

TABLE 1. SUMMARY DIGEST OF STATE ENABLING ACTS GRANTING TO LOCAL UNITS POWERS OVER RECREATION SYSTEMS

Key to Recreation Facilities: a, Playgrounds; b, Play Fields; c, Recreation Centers; d, Swimming Pools; e, Bathing Beaches; f, Golf Courses; g, Camps; h, Public Baths; i, Gymnasiums; j, Parks; k, Public Gardens; l, Other Recreation Activities and Facilities

State	Year Enacted	Governmental Units Affected	Authority Vested In	How Lands and Buildings to be Used for Recreation are to be Obtained	Recreation Facilities over which Powers Extend	Cooperation with School Board	Provision for Joint Conduct	How Instituted	Maintenance	Separate Fund for all Recreation Money	Tax to be in addition to all other taxes city may levy
Connecticut	1923	town, city, borough			a, c, d, h, i, j, k				approp.		
Florida	1925	municipality, county	school bd., park bd., existing body, or playground and recreation bd.	use of prop. owned or leased by munic., bond issues, acquisition by lawful means, gifts	a, c, l		two or more municipalities, or counties, school dist. and munic.	5% of voters, popular ref., incl. tax levy of 1/2 to 1 mill	tax levy	x	
Georgia	1923	cities, towns	school bd., park bd., existing body, or playground and recreation bd.	gift, use of property owned or leased by munic. bond issues	a, c, k		two or more municipalities, school bd. and munic.	10% of voters, popular ref., incl. tax limit of one mill	tax, gifts	x	
Illinois	1921 am. 1923 1925 1927	city, town, village, less than 150,000 pop.	school bd., park bd., existing body or rec. bd.	gift, use of municipally owned or leased prop., bond issues, approp.	a, c		two or more munic. park bd., school bd. and munic.	pop. ref., 10% of voters, max. tax 2/3 of one mill	tax, gifts		tax for recreation to be in addition to taxable limit of munic.

State	Year	Units	Administering body	Powers	Letters	Cooperation	Joint units	Referendum	Finance	
Indiana	1925 am. 1927	cities, 3rd, 4th, 5th class; towns	bd. of school trustees, existing bd., recreation bd.	use of mun. prop., lease, purchase, condemnation	a, b, c, d, e, g, h, i, l	one member of rec. bd. to be mem. of school bd., school property may be placed at disposal of rec. bd.	two or more municip., munic. and sch. corp.	pop. ref., 10% of those voting at last election	tax levy max. 3 mills	x
Iowa	1915 am. 1924	cities	playground commission	acquisition, use of mun. property, condemnation	a, c	joint mainten. by city and school bd. where possible		pop. ref., 15% of those voting at last election	tax levy max. 2 mills	x
Kentucky	1924	cities, counties	park bd., bd. of educ., existing body, or playground and rec. bd.	use of mun. property, purchase, lease, condemnation	a, c		two or more cities, city and county, or city or county and school board		gifts, appropriation	x
Louisiana	1924	cities, towns, villages, parishes	park bd., school bd., existing bd., or playground and rec. bd.	use of mun. property, acquisition, lease	a, c, l		two or more political subdivisions, school bd. and political unit		gifts, appropriation	x
Massachusetts	1919	cities, towns	park bd., school bd., or playground and rec. comm. or together	gift, lease, purchase, condemnation	a, c				appropriation	
Michigan	1917	cities, villages, counties, townships	local govt., recreation bd.	use of mun. property, private prop. with consent of owners	a, l		political unit may unite with school board or other units		appropriation	

TABLE I—*Continued*

State	Year Enacted	Govern-mental Units Affected	Authority Vested In	How Lands and Buildings to be Used for Recreation are to be Obtained	Recreation Facilities over which Powers Extend	Cooperation with School Board	Provision for Joint Conduct	How Instituted	Main-tenance	Separate Fund for all Recreation Money	Tax to be in addition to all other taxes city may levy
New Hampshire	1917	cities, towns	park bd., school bd., recreation commission, or a combination	use of mun. property, gift, lease, condemnation	a, c, d, h, l	recreation activities may be carried on in school prop. subject to control by school bd.			appropriation		
New Jersey	1911 am. 1915 1925	cities, towns, townships, boroughs, villages, counties	bd. of recreation commissioners	gift, purchase, lease, condemnation	a, b, c, d, h, i		two or more political units	pop. ref., 15% of voters at last election, incl. tax levy	admission fees, tax levy	x	
New York	1917 am. 1924	cities 2nd and 3rd class, towns, villages, counties outside New York except Erie	school bd., park bd., existing bd. or recreation commission	use of mun. property, gift, purchase, lease, condemnation	a, c, d, h	presidents of school bd. and park bd. ex-officio members of commission	two or more municipalities, school bd. and munic.	pop. ref., 5% of voters at last gubernatorial election, incl. tax levy not exceeding 2 mills	tax levy, appropriation	x	
North Carolina	1923	cities, towns, townships, school districts, counties	school bd., park bd., recreation commission	use of mun. property, gift, purchase, lease, condemnation	a, c, l		two or more municipalities	pop. ref., 25% of voters, incl. tax	tax levy, gifts	x	tax for recreation in addition to taxable limit of municipality
Ohio	1921	cities, villages, counties	existing body, recreation board	use of mun. prop., or acquisition by lawful means	a, b, c, d, h, i	two members of school bd. to be members of rec. bd.	two or more political units; school bd. and pol. unit		appropriation		

State	Date	Administering body	Powers	Activities	Board composition	Units	Referendum	Financing		Notes
Pennsylvania	1919 am. 1921 1927	cities 2nd and 3rd class, boroughs, counties, townships	existing bd., recreation bd.	use of mun. prop., gift, purchase, lease, condemnation	a, b, c, d, h, i, j, l	two members of school bd. to be members of rec. bd.	two or more political units; school bd. and pol. unit		appropriation		
Rhode Island	1924	cities, towns	school committee, park bd., or recreation bd.	use of mun. property, gift, purchase, lease	a, b, c, d, e, l	member of school comm. and park bd. may be ex-officio members of rec. bd.	two or more political units		appropriation		
Utah	1923	cities, 1st, 2nd and 3rd class, towns, school districts, counties	existing bd., recreation bd.	use of mun. property, acquisition by lawful means	a, b, c, d, g, h, i, l	two members of school bd. to be members of recreation bd.	school dist. and town, city or county		appropriation, gifts	x	
Vermont	1925	cities, towns, villages, school districts	existing bd., school bd., bureau of rec., or rec. bd.	use of mun. property, gift, purchase, lease, condemnation	a		two or more political units	pop. ref., initiated by 50 voters or governing body, incl. sum to be appropriated	tax levy		
Virginia	1924	cities, towns, counties	existing bd., bureau of rec., school bd., or recreation bd.	use of mun. property, gift, purchase, lease, condemnation	a, l		two or more political units	pop. ref., initiated by 10% of voters, incl. tax not exceeding 2 mills	tax levy		
West Virginia	1925	cities, towns, counties, school districts	existing bd., bureau of rec., school bd., or recreation bd.	use of mun. property, gift, purchase, lease, condemnation	a, l	school bd. to be represented on rec. bd.	two or more units including school districts	pop. ref., initiated by 20% of voters at last election, incl. tax not exceeding 3 mills	tax levy		tax for recreation in addition to taxable limit of municipality

Local Laws

As in the case of the state laws, there is no such thing as a model ordinance making provision for the establishment of a local recreation system. On account of the diversity of the state laws on the subject and the difference in local conditions, no single law will meet all the needs. However the Playground and Recreation Association in giving assistance to Illinois cities which were considering the creation of recreation boards drafted a suggested ordinance, a copy of which is here set forth. The main provisions of this law cover what should be included in such an ordinance as discovered from experience in various localities. It includes such subjects as:

> Organization of the Board
> Recreation Facilities over which the Board is to have
> > jurisdiction
> Powers and Duties
> > Cooperation with School, Park, and other governmental agencies
> > Power to receive gifts, donations, etc.
> > Power to conduct recreation outside the city limits
> Maintenance
> > Tax Levy, amount specified
> Creation of Separate Fund for Recreation Income
> Tax Levy to be in addition to the taxable limit of the
> > municipality.

An Ordinance Providing for the Establishment, Maintenance and Conduct of a Playground and Recreation System

Be it ordained by the city council of the City of ....:

Section 1. There is hereby established a Playground and Recreation Board for the City of ...., composed of three members, to be appointed by the mayor, by and with the consent of the council. Of the members first appointed, one shall be appointed for a term of three years, one for a term of two years and one for a term of one year. Subsequent appointments shall be made for three year terms. Members shall serve until their successors are appointed and qualified. In case of vacancy the mayor shall appoint a successor to serve for the unexpired term. The members of the board shall serve without compensation. A majority of the members shall constitute a quorum for the transaction of business. The Board shall elect necessary officers and adopt such rules, by-laws and regulations as it may deem proper for the conduct of its work.

Section 2. The Playground and Recreation Board shall have power to maintain and equip playgrounds and recreation centers and the buildings thereon, within or beyond the corporate limits of the City of ...., and may for the purposes of carrying out the purposes for which this ordinance is adopted, employ play leaders, playground directors, supervisors, recreation superintendents or such other officers or employees as they deem proper. Such Board shall have and may exercise all powers conferred by " An Act to provide for the acquisition, equipment, conduct and maintenance of public playgrounds and recreation centers in and by cities, towns and villages of less than one hundred fifty thousand inhabitants," in force July 1, 1921, as subsequently amended. In the exercise of the powers conferred by such act and by this ordinance, the Board may co-operate or join with school, park and other governmental authorities and bodies, and shall have power to use lands, buildings and equipment made available to it by other governmental bodies and authorities.

Section 2. The Playground and Recreation Board may accept any grant or devise of real estate or any gift or bequest of money or other personal property or any donation, the principal or income of which is to be applied for either temporary or permanent use for playground or recreation purposes; but if the acceptance thereof for such purposes shall subject the City of .... to expense for improvements, maintenance or renewal, the acceptance of any grant or devise of real estate shall

be subject to the approval of the city council of such city.
Money received for such purpose, unless otherwise provided by
the terms of the gift or bequest, shall be deposited with the
treasurer of the City of .... to the account of the Playground and Recreation Board, and such money may be withdrawn and paid out upon warrants drawn upon the municipal
treasury by such Playground and Recreation Board.

Section 4. The city council of the City of .... shall
annually levy and collect a tax of not less than ...., nor
more than one and one-third mills on each dollar of assessed
valuation of all taxable property within the corporate limits of
such city, such tax to be designated as " Playground and Recreation Tax ", and to be levied and collected in like manner as the
general tax for this city is collected. Such tax shall be in addition
to the maximum of taxes permitted to such city, and exclusive
of all other taxes such city may levy or collect, and shall not be
scaled down. The cost and expense incurred by the Playground
and Recreation Board shall be paid out of the taxes so collected,
or out of money received as, or realized from, gifts received for
this purpose, and the same shall be expended under the direction of such Board and shall be paid out upon the warrants
drawn on the municipal treasury upon order of such Board.

In the following summary digest of local laws embracing
sixty cities of various sizes and in different parts of the
country, an effort has been made to get all possible shades
of difference in the legal aspect of public provisions for
recreation. The categories under which the provisions of
the laws were grouped are similar to those of the main features of the ordinance suggested by the Playground and
Recreation Association. The population of the cities was
included in order to show that representatives of all classes
of cities had been selected. The law was classified as to
whether it was a local ordinance, a charter provision, or a
special state law, or an ordinance carrying into effect a special
state law. In some cases, the provisions seem to be rather

meagre. This may be due to the fact that the local ordinance is simply a statement of the fact that the municipality is carrying into effect the grant of powers made in the state home-rule enabling act. In other cases, the provisions may be very full, indicating that the state within which the municipality is located has no such state law. Under the head of Maintenance, it is not to be assumed that when no entry is made, there is no provision for maintenance of the recreational activities. It may merely mean that the local law does not specifically provide the method of maintenance. In such cases, appropriation is the usual method, although it would be necessary to know the provisions of the state law of the state in which the city is located.

TABLE 2. SUMMARY DIGEST OF MUNICIPAL ORDINANCES AND CHARTER PROVISIONS COVERING PUBLIC RECREATION

Key to Facilities: a, Parks; b, Playgrounds; c, Parkways; d, Boulevards; e, Athletic Fields; f, Bathing Beaches; g, Swimming Pools; h, Golf Courses; i, Recreation Centers; j, Community Music; k, Plays, Celebrations, etc.; l, Stadia; m, Gymnasiums; n, Summer Camps; o, Bath Houses; p, Dance Halls; q, Auditoriums

City	Population 1920	Ordinance	Charter Provision	Special State Law	Adopted	Power Vested in	Number Members	Term	Appointed by	School Board and Park Board Represented	Supervision over Recreational Facilities	Additional Powers	Maintenance	Miscellaneous Provisions
California:														
Chico	9,339		x		1921	Bidwell Park and Playground Commissioners	5	4 yrs.	City Council		a, b	may receive gifts, donations. etc.		
Glendale	13,536	x			1926	Park, Playground and Recreation Commission	5	3 yrs.	Council		a, b, e, f, g, i, j, k	appoint Supt. of Parks and Recreation with consent of Council	appropriation	
Sacramento	65,908		x		1921	Supt. of Recreation			City Manager		a, and all places of recreation		appropriation	all moneys raised for recreation to be kept in separate fund
Los Angeles	576,673		x		1924	Board of Playground Commissioners	5	4 yrs.	Mayor with consent of Council		b, h, i	receive donations, legacies, bequests	appropriation	separate fund for playground revenues

APPENDIX A (182)

City	Population			Date est.	Administrative body	No.	Term	Appointed by	Ex-officio members	Facilities	Powers	Financing
Colorado: Denver	256,491	x		1904 am. 1912	Manager of Improvements and Parks			Mayor		a, b, c, mountain parks		annual tax at least 1⅓ mills
Connecticut: Bridgeport	143,555	x		1917	Recreation Commission	5	4 yrs.	3 appointed by head of govt.	Members of School Bd. and Park Bd. members of Comm.	b, e, f, g, i, j, k, o, p	conduct rec. activities on park and school prop., and prop. not owned by city with consent of owners	
Bristol	20,620	x		1924 rev.	Board of Park Commissioners	6		Head of govt.		a, b, c, d	receive donations, gifts, etc., may carry on rec. activities outside city limits	
Hartford	138,036	x		1895	Board of Park Commissioners	10	7 yrs.	Board with consent of Council		a, b, c, d	condemnation, receive gifts, donations, bequests, etc.	tax levy, max. ½ mill, bond issues, max. $300,000
Florida: Jacksonville	91,558		x	1927	Playground and Recreation Board	5	2 yrs.	Mayor		b, g, h, i, l	receive gifts, donations, etc.	pop. ref. initiated by 10% of voters to levy tax of ½ to 1 mill
St. Petersburg	14,237	x		1924	Public Recreation Board	5		Board of City Commissioners		b, e, j, n, or other facilities	may conduct rec. on school prop., park prop., or private prop. with consent of owners	appropriation

TABLE 2—*Continued*

City	Population 1920	Ordinance	Charter Provision	Special State Law	Adopted	Power Vested in	Organization				Powers and Duties		Maintenance	Miscellaneous Provisions
							Number Members	Term	Appointed by	School Board and Park Board Represented	Supervision over Recreational Facilities	Additional Powers		
Tampa	51,608	x			1924	Board of Public Rec.	5	4 yrs.	Mayor-Commissioner with consent of City Commission	Member of Park Bd. to member of Rec. Bd.	b, e, f, g, h, i	conduct rec. activities on property not owned by city with consent of owners	appropriation	
Winter Haven	3403	x			1926	Public Recreation Board	5	5 yrs.	Mayor-Commissioner with consent of City Comm.		b, e, f, g, h, i	conduct rec. activities on property not owned by city with consent of owners	appropriation	
Georgia: Columbus	31,125	x			1925	Park and Recreation Bd.	5	5 yrs.	City Commission		a, b, and recreation system	conduct recreation on school property, receive donations, legacies, bequests, and recommend condemnation proceedings	appropriation	separate fund for recreation money

City	Population		Year	Organization	No.	Term	Appointed by / Head of City Govt.	Ex-officio members	(b)	Powers	Support	Remarks
Macon	52,995	x			3	2 yrs.	Mayor and Council		b, e, f, g, j, k, l	receive donations, acquire leasehold interest in lands	appropriation	
Idaho: Lewiston	6,574	x	1918	Board of Public Recreation under Dept. of Public Property	5	4 yrs.	Mayor with consent of Council		b	receive gifts of real estate or money, cooperate with school bd. and other governmental agencies, conduct recreation outside city limits	tax levy, not less than 2/3 nor more than 1 1/3 mills, gifts	separate fund for recreation money, tax levy to be in addition to taxable limit of municipality
Illinois: Centralia	12,491	x	1924	Playground and Recreation Board	5	3 yrs.			b, i			
Galesburg	23,834	x	1916	Board of Public Recreation	7	5 yrs.	one by Mayor, one by Council, one by School Bd., and two by five members	Member of School Board and member of Park Board to be members	b, f, g, i, j, k	use school prop., park prop., and private prop. with consent of owners	appropriation	
Peoria	76,121	x	1916	Board of Public Recreation	7	5 yrs.	Mayor appoints four	Supt. of Schools, member of Park Bd. to be members	b, e, f, g, i, j k	use school and park prop., also private prop., with consent of owners; may take lands in fee, or by gift, purchase, condemnation, or lease	appropriation	

TABLE 2—*Continued*

City	Population 1920	Ordinance	Charter Provision	Special State Law	Adopted	Power Vested in	Number Members	Term	Appointed by	School Board and Park Board Represented	Supervision over Recreational Facilities	Additional Powers	Maintenance	Miscellaneous Provisions
Springfield	59,183	x			1924	Playground and Recreation Board	5	5 yrs.	Head of govt.		b, c	conduct rec. activities on prop. of school bd. and park bd.; conduct recreation outside city limits; receive gifts, donations, etc.	tax levy, not less than ⅔, nor more than 1⅓ mills	
Iowa Des Moines	126,468	x			1920	Playground Commission	5	6 yrs.	City Council			to act in advisory capacity with several departments of city govt. in all playground and recreation matters		
Kentucky: Bowling Green	9,638	x			1925	Board of Parks and Playgrounds	5	5 yrs.	Head of govt.		a, b, i	receive gifts, donations, etc.	appropriation of $5oo.oo	

State / City	Population			Date	Park Commission		Term	Head of govt.				appropriation	
Louisiana: Shreveport	43,874	x		1922		9	2 yrs.		a, b, c, d	b, f, i, k			
Maine: Portland	69,272		x	1915	Recreation Comm.	7	1 yr.		one member of school committee, one member of park commission			12½ per cent of appropriation for parks to be paid by park commission to rec. commission	City Council is recreation commission under change in Portland's charter to council-manager govt.
Massachusetts: Boston	748,060	x	x	rev. 1925	Park Dept.	3							
Fall River	120,485	x	x	1924	Recreation Commission	5	5 yrs.	Head of govt. with consent of Council	member of school and park boards, members of rec. comm.	a, b, c, f, j, m, o	general supervision over play and recreation		
Somerville	93,091	x		1921	Public Welfare and Recreation Commission	10	2 yrs.	Mayor with consent of Board of Aldermen		general supervision			
Waltham	30,915		x	1914	Board of Recreation	5	3 yrs.	Mayor	members of school and park boards, members of rec. comm.	b, f, i, k, m	may assume charge of school playgrounds and school bldgs. for rec. purposes on request of school comm., may have supervision of dance halls, moving picture shows and other forms of commercial recreation	appropriation	

TABLE 2—*Continued*

City	Population 1920	Ordinance	Charter Provision	Special State Law	Adopted	Power Vested in	Organization				Powers and Duties		Maintenance	Miscellaneous Provisions
							Number Members	Term	Appointed by	School Board and Park Board Represented	Supervision over Recreational Facilities	Additional Powers		
Michigan: Grand Rapids	137,634		x		1916	Director of Public Welfare					general supervision incl. parks			
Pontiac	34,273		x		1920	Director of Public Welfare					general supervision, a, b			
Minnesota: Minneapolis	380,582		x		rev. 1925	Board of Park Commissioners					a, b, c, e, f, i,	may issue bonds, the interest on which must not exceed $35,000 annually, must levy annual tax for playgrounds not to exceed $\frac{1}{4}$ mill	bond issues, tax levy	
Missouri: Kansas City	324,410		x		1925	Division of Recreation under Director of Welfare					b, f, g, and other rec. facilities	supervision of commercial recreation, may conduct rec. on property of park dept, subject to its rules and regulations		

APPENDIX A (188)

City	Population			Year	Administrative Body	No.	Term	Appointed by	Other Member	Activities	Provisions	Support
St. Louis	772,897	x		1917	Commissioner of Parks and Recreation					a, b, i, j, o		appropriation, donations
Nebraska: Omaha	191,601	x		1915	Board of Recreation	5	4 yrs.	City Council	Supt. of Parks and Public Property a member of Board of Rec.	l, e, f, g, i, k, m, o, and related activities	may conduct rec. on school and park prop. subject to those boards, may use private prop. when loaned for that purpose	
New Hampshire Keene	11,210		x	rev. 1924	Playground Commission	3		Head of govt.		b, e		
Manchester	78,384		x	comp. 1924	Dept. of Parks, Commons, and Playgrounds	5	5 yrs.	Head of govt.		a, b, c, and commons		
New York Lackawanna	17,918	x		1924	Recreation Comm. in Dept. of Public Works	5	5 yrs.	Head of govt.		b, i		
Port Chester	16,573	x		1917	Recreation Commission	5		Head of govt.	Supt. of Public Schools a member	b, i, j, k, o, and all other rec. activities	may use school prop. and private prop. for rec. with consent of owners	appropriation
Rochester	295,750		x	1915	Supt. Bureau of Recreation and Playgrounds under Commissioner of Parks					b, e, g, o	may conduct rec. on school prop. at request of Board of Education	

TABLE 2—*Continued*

City	Population 1920	Ordinance	Charter Provision	Special State Law	Adopted	Power Vested in	Number Members	Term	Appointed by	School Board and Park Board Represented	Supervision over Recreational Facilities	Additional Powers	Maintenance	Miscellaneous Provisions
								Organization			Powers and Duties			
Ohio: Cleveland	796,841		x		mun. code 1924	Division of Recreation in Dept. of Parks and Public Prop.					b, e, h, o, p, and general supervision			
Lima	41,326	x			1924	Recreation Board	5	5 yrs.	Mayor	two members of Board of Educ. to be members of Rec. Board	b, e, g, i, m, o	may conduct rec. on school prop. in cooperation with School Board		
Mansfield	27,824	x			1924	Recreation Board	5	5 yrs.	Mayor	two members of School Board to be members of Rec. Bd.	b, e. g, i, m, o	may conduct rec. on school prop. in cooperation with School Board		
Steubenville	28,508	x			1924	Recreation Board	5	5 yrs.	Mayor	two members of School Board members of Rec. Bd.	b, e, g, i, m, o	may unite with school district in conducting rec.		

City	Population		Year	Board	No.	Term	Appointed by	Composition	Powers	Finance	Support
Wellsville	8,849	x	1924	Public Recreation Board	5	5 yrs.	Mayor	two members of School Board to be members of Rec. Bd.	b, e, g, i, m, o	may receive gifts, donations, etc., power extends over rec. outside city limits	
Oklahoma: Bartlesville	14,417	x	rev. ord. 1924	Board of Park Commissioners	3	3 yrs.	Head of govt.		a, b, c, d		appropriation
Tulsa	72,075	x	1908	Park Board	4	2 yrs.	Head of govt.		a	tax of 1/10 of 1%	
Oregon: Klamath Falls	4,801	x	1924	Public Recreation Commission	5	1 yr.	Mayor with approv. of Council		b, e, f, i, j, k, and recreation of every kind	may receive gifts, donations, etc.	appropriation
Pennsylvania: Coatesville	14,415	x	1917	Parks and Playground Commission in Dept. of Parks and Public Prop.	3			Supt. of Parks & Pub. Prop. and one member appointed by School Dist, third member chosen by these two	a, b		appropriation, part of which to be paid by School District
Johnstown	67,327	x	1917	Board of Public Recreation in Dept. of Parks and Public Prop.	5	3 yrs.	two by City Council	Supt. Parks and Public Prop., and one member appointed by School Dist, fifth member chosen by these four	general supervision	may conduct rec. on school prop. with consent of School Dist, also on private prop. with consent of owner	appropriation

TABLE 2—Continued

| City | Population 1920 | Ordinance | Charter Provision | Special State Law | Adopted | Power Vested in | Organization | | | | Powers and Duties | | Maintenance | Miscellaneous Provisions |
							Number Members	Term	Appointed by	School Board and Park Board Represented	Supervision over Recreational Facilities	Additional Powers		
Phoenixville	10,484	x			1920	Recreation Board	5	5 yrs.	Burgess	two members of School Board to be members of Rec. Bd.	b, e, g, i, m		tax in 1920 of ½ of 1 mill; an equal sum to be appropriated by school district or ordinance becomes null and void	
Philadelphia	1,823,779		x		1918	Director of Public Welfare					b, f, i, o, and general supervision	may assume charge of school vacation playgrounds when requested by school authorities		
Pittsburgh	588,343	x			1915	Bureau of Rec. in Dept. of Public Works					b			
Scranton	137,783	x			1922	Bureau of Recreation	7	3 yrs.	Mayor	one member of School Bd.	a, b, e, g, k, m, n, o	may conduct rec. on school prop. and on prop. of Dept. of Public Works with consent of these Depts.	appropriation	

City	Population			Year estab.	Name of Board	No.	Term	Appointed by	Composition	Powers (general)	Powers (conduct)	Support	Notes
Rhode Island: Newport	30,255	x		1915	Board of Recreation	9	2 yrs.	Mayor	one member of Park Bd. and one from School Bd. to be members	general supervision	may conduct rec. on school, park, and private prop., with consent of owners, may receive gifts, donations, etc.	appropriation	
Texas: Forth Worth	106,482		x	1922	Public Recreation Board	5	5 yrs.	Head of govt.		b, e, g, h, i, j, k, and general supervision	may conduct rec. on school and park property, may receive gifts, donations, etc., may conduct rec. outside city limits	tax levy, 2 to 5 mills	
Galveston	44,255		x	1919	Board of Supervisors of Parks and Playgrounds	3	2 yrs.	City Council		a, b			
Houston	138,276		x	1921	Dept. of Recreation and Community Service	11	2 yrs.	Head of govt.	member of School and Park Boards to be members of Dept.	b, e, i, m, o, and general supervision	may conduct rec. on school, park, and private prop. with consent of owners, may receive gifts, donations, etc.	appropriation	separate fund for recreation money

TABLE 2—*Continued*

City	Population 1920	Ordinance	Charter Provision	Special State Law	Adopted	Power Vested in	Organization				Powers and Duties		Maintenance	Miscellaneous Provisions
							Number Members	Term	Appointed by	School Board and Park Board Represented	Supervision over Recreational Facilities	Additional Powers		
Waco	38,500		x		1923	Public Recreation Board	5	5 yrs.	Board of Commissioners		b, e, and other rec. facilities	may conduct rec. on school prop. with consent of School Board, may conduct rec. outside city limits	appropriation	board to have exclusive control of all funds set aside for its use or coming from bond issues for rec.
Utah: Salt Lake City	118,110	x			rev. ord. 1920	Supervisor of Playgrounds in Dept. of Parks and Public Prop.			Board of Commissioners		b			
Virginia: Norfolk	115,777		x		1920	Bureau of Rec. and Charities in Dept. of Public Welfare					a, b, and general supervision	regulation of amusements and entertainments		
Wisconsin: Bangor	854	x			1924	Park Board	5	5 yrs.	Pres. of Village Board with approval of Board		a, b, c, d, pleasure drives and rec. grounds	may acquire prop. by gift, purchase, devise, bequest, or condemnation	appropriation	separate fund known as Park Fund

APPENDIX B

MODEL ORDINANCE PREPARED BY THE LEAGUE OF KANSAS
MUNICIPALITIES AS A GUIDE TO MUNICIPALITIES
CONSIDERING THE CREATION OF MUNICIPAL
TOURIST CAMPS

AN ORDINANCE CREATING A MOTORISTS' TOURIST CAMP,
PROVIDING FOR THE REGULATION THEREOF AND
ESTABLISHING A FEE FOR PERMITS
TO CAMP THEREIN

Be it Ordained by the Governing Body of the city of ......
...., Kansas.

Motorists' Tourist Camp Created. Section 1. That there is
hereby created and established a motorists' tourist camp on
Lots .... in Blocks ....
in the .... Subdivision of this city which
shall be or constitute a part of the city park system.

Camp Facilities. Section 2. That said camp shall be divided
into camp sites, lanes, and drives and that there shall be constructed in said tourist camp such conveniences as the governing body of this city may order, *provided* that the camp shall be
properly lighted at the expense of the city, and that reasonable
quantites of water for drinking, bathing, and sanitary purposes,
and sanitary facilities shall be furnished to those persons who
secure permits to camp therein.

Custodian and Assistant Custodian. Section 3. That there be
and is hereby created the office of custodian of the motorists'
tourist camp. Such custodian shall be appointed by the Mayor
by and with the consent of the governing body of this city and
said custodian shall hold office at the pleasure of the Mayor.
The Mayor shall likewise have power to appoint such assistant

custodians as may from time to time be necessary in the same manner as provided for the appointment of the custodian, *provided,* that any police officer of the city may be appointed custodian or assistant custodian and *provided further* that all persons appointed to the position of custodian or assistant custodian who are not at the time of their appointment police officers, shall be deputized by the Mayor as such and shall be and remain special police officers during the tenure of their office as custodian or assistant custodian of said motorists' tourist camp.

Powers and Duties of Custodian. Section 4. That the custodian of the motorists' tourist camp shall enforce all city ordinances and rules for the government and use of the camp both within and without said camp. He shall maintain peace and order and proper sanitary conditions in the camp. He shall be the city's special representative to receive the tourists and promote their comfort and happiness with all the conveniences provided by the city in the camp. He shall be on duty at such hours as the Mayor may direct and shall receive as compensation for his services the sum of $.... per month. Assistant custodians shall assist the custodian in the performance of the duties set forth in this ordinance and in the absence of the custodian shall perform his duties. They shall be on duty such hours as the mayor may prescribe and shall receive as compensation for their services the sum of $.... per month.

Sales in Camp. Section 5. That it shall be unlawful for any person, firm, or corporation to place advertisements and posters in the tourist camp or locate any concessions or stands for the purpose of selling foods, drinks or supplies and equipment without first securing a license from the mayor and city clerk to carry on such calling or transact such business and paying the fee therefor as prescribed by ordinance.

Registration of Tourists. Section 6. That any person in charge of an automobile or other vehicle shall, immediately upon arriving in the tourist camp, and before pitching camp or otherwise establishing himself or his party in said camp, register in a tourist camp register to be provided by the city, the date of arrival, his name, the number in his party, his home address, his destination, vehicle engine number, vehicle body number, license number, and the kind of vehicle, and shall procure at once, and before or at the expiration of each twenty-four hour period thereafter, from the tourist camp custodian, a camping permit, for which said person shall pay to the custodian, fifty cents, and receive therefor a tourist camp tag receipt and identification card. Such tourist camp tag shall be tied on the steering wheel or steering apparatus of the vehicle, *provided* that the tourist camp custodian may refuse to grant a permit to camp to any person who, in his judgment, is not a desirable guest of the camp or may revoke any permit for like reasons, *provided* that such person who is refused a permit or whose permit is revoked may appeal from the decision of the custodian to the mayor of this city. *Provided further* that any person may secure not to exceed two additional camping permits at fifty cents each under which he may occupy not to exceed two additional camp sites whenever said additional camp sites are available *provided further* that the city hereby reserves the right to cancel said additional camping permits, refunding the fee paid therefor, whenever in the judgment of the custodian the crowded condition of the camp demands the same.

Assignment of Camp Sites. Section 7. That all persons who have procured a permit to camp in the tourist camp as provided in section four thereof shall be assigned by the custodian to a camp site and shall not move any of their equipment beyond the bounds of such camp site or trespass upon the camp sites occupied by other persons.

Guests to Observe Ordinances and Rules. Section 8. That all persons sojourning in said camp shall observe all the ordinances of this city and all rules and regulations governing the use of this camp.

Animals. Section 9. That it shall be unlawful for any person or persons to bring into the tourist camp any horse, cow, or hog, and all other animals brought into the camp shall be securely chained on the camp site of their harborers in such a manner that they cannot trespass on any other camp site.

Rules and Ordinances Available. Section 10. That each

person registering in the camp may receive a copy of this ordinance and all rules and regulations governing the use of this camp, and a copy of this ordinance and such rules and regulations shall be posted in a conspicuous place in the camp; *provided* that an accessible copy of the city ordinances shall be kept for the use of the campers by the custodian of the camp.

Rules of the Camp. Section 11. That the following rules are hereby adopted for the further regulation of the tourist camp:—

A. The maximum length of stay in the camp shall be three days, except in cases of bad weather and sickness, *provided* the custodian may grant additional permits for good and sufficient reason.

B. Only portable shelters shall be erected on any camp site by any person without the authority of the governing body of this city.

C. No person shall reside in this tourist camp while actively engaged in any regular labor in this community.

D. No person residing in this camp shall offer for sale or sell any goods or take orders for future delivery within the limits of this camp.

E. No speeches, addresses or sermons shall be delivered nor any doctrine proclaimed publicly in this tourist camp unless a permit so to do has been obtained from the mayor and city clerk of this city.

F. All persons occupying camp sites in this tourist camp shall refrain from throwing any trash, litter or other things in any of the lanes or drives in this camp and such persons shall clean up all trash, litter or other material or things which they have deposited on their camp site, or permitted to be deposited there, before leaving such camp site.

G. All refuse, trash, litter or other discarded thing must be put in the containers provided by the city and the lid replaced securely.

H. No person having any fire in any stove, oven, or fire place shall leave the same ungarded at any time.

I. No person shall dig any hole, cut or otherwise destroy any turf or grass in this camp and no oil or grease shall be poured out in any place within the limits of the camp except as permitted by the custodian.

J. No person shall mutilate, destroy or molest any tree or public property in this tourist camp or mutilate, destroy or molest any private property not his own, in this camp.

K. No person shall register under any fictitious name or otherwise register falsely in the tourist-camp registry book.

L. No person shall counterfeit any camping permit issued by this city or its authorized representative.

Responsibility of City. Section 12. That this city will not be responsible for any property lost, stolen, or damaged in the tourist camp.

Penalty. Section 13. That any person or persons who shall violate any of the rules and regulations provided in this ordinance shall, upon conviction thereof, be deemed guilty of a misdemeanor and shall be punished by a fine of not less than $1.00, nor more than $100.00, and costs, or by imprisonment in the city jail for not less than one day nor more than thirty days, or by both such fine and imprisonment and in event of non-payment of fine or costs or both, shall be committed to the city jail until such fine and costs are paid.

Take Effect. Section 14. That this ordinance shall take effect and be in full force from and after its publication according to law.

APPENDIX C

STATE LAWS EMPOWERING MUNICIPALITIES TO
SPEND PUBLIC FUNDS FOR MUSIC

TABLE 3. SUMMARY DIGEST OF PROVISIONS OF STATE LAWS COVERING MUNICIPAL BAND CONCERTS AND MUNICIPAL MUSIC

State	Year Enacted	Governmental Units Affected	Provisions For	Tax Levy (Maximum)	Appropriation	Popular Referendum	Tax to be in addition to taxable limit of munic.	Miscellaneous Provisions
Alabama	1919	cities, towns, counties	band concerts, music		x			
Arizona	1927	cities, towns	band concerts	.001		initiated by 10% voters		
California	1911	cities, except freeholder charter cities	music	.001½		init. by gov. body	x	
Colorado	1917	cities, towns	music	.000$\frac{6}{10}$	x			
Idaho	1927	all municipalities	band concerts	.002		init. by 10% voters		
Illinois	1925 am. 1927	cities towns, villages, less than 500,000 pop.	band concerts	.001		init. by 5% voters	x	
Indiana	1923 am. 1927	cities, towns	music		$1,200.00			
Iowa	1921	cities, towns, less than 40,000 pop.	band concerts	.002		init. by 10% voters		
Kansas	1925	cities, townships	band concerts	.000½		init. by 20% voters		
Kentucky	1926	cities (4th, 5th, 6th class)	band concerts	.002		init. by 5% voters		
Maine	1927	cities, towns	band concerts			x		
Massachusetts	1904 am. 1908	towns	band concerts, music		$500.00			may raise money
Michigan	1923	cities, villages, counties, less than 50,000 pop.	band concerts	.002		init. by 10% voters		

State	Date	Units	Purpose	Tax rate	Maximum amount	Initiative and referendum	levy not to be made if there is an unexpended balance in treasury amounting to maximum levy
Minnesota	1927	cities (2nd, 3rd, 4th class), villages	band concerts	.002	$10,000.00	init. by 10% voters	
Mississippi	1912	municipalities	band concerts		$1,200.00		
Missouri	1927	cities, towns, villages, less than 25,000 pop.	band concerts	.001		gov. body may levy .000½; more than that by pop. ref., init. by 10% voters	
Montana	1917 am. 1923	cities (1st, 2nd, 3rd class), towns	band concerts	.001			
Nebraska	comp. stat. 1922, 1927	cities, towns, villages	band concerts, music	.001			
Nevada	1927	cities, towns	band concerts	.000½		init. by 10% voters	
New Hampshire	rev. laws 1925	towns	band concerts		$800.00		referendum does not apply if city or village has charter provision for band
New York	1923	cities (1st, 2nd, 3rd class), villages	band concerts	.001 in cities with property valuation under $15,000,000; in others .000½		init. by gov. body in cities of 1st and 2nd class; city or village of 3rd class, init. by 5% voters	
North Dakota	1927	cities, villages	band concerts			init. by 10% voters	
Ohio	Code 1925	municipalities	band concerts		$1,000.00		
Pennsylvania	1925	boroughs	music	.001			
South Dakota	1923	cities, towns	music	.001		init. by 20% voters	
Texas	1925	cities, towns	band concerts	.003		init. by 10% voters	creation of non-partisan committee of three to five members to formulate rules concerning band

TABLE 3—*Continued*

State	Year Enacted	Governmental Units Affected	Provisions For	Tax Levy (Maximum)	Appropriation	Popular Referendum	Tax to be in addition to taxable limit of munic.	Miscellaneous Provisions
Utah	1923	cities	music					connected with recreation program
Vermont	1917	cities, towns, villages	music	5% of grand list if that does not exceed $20,000, otherwise 3%				
W. Virginia	1923	incorporated municipalities	band concerts	.00½				municipalities over 2000 incorporated by state law, power over band concerts must be covered by charter provision
Wisconsin	1919	towns, villages, cities	public concerts					appropriation to cover deficit

APPENDIX C (204)

APPENDIX D

State Laws Making Provisions for State Parks, Forests and Reservations

When one considers that the Conservation Law of New York State fills a volume of 560 pages, while the Pennsylvania Game, Fish and Forest Laws fill another volume of 330 pages, it would be an ambitious procedure to attempt to make a summary digest of the provisions of all the state laws on the subjects of parks, forests and reservations. The purpose, however, of the following digest is not that of providing a ready reference table for all the provisions of all the state laws bearing on these subjects. It is, rather, to show the wide diversity of legislation existing among the states. To this end, such of the provisions are included as reveal the differences in (1) administrative organization; (2) general powers and duties of the board or boards; (3) methods of maintenance; and other provisions of a general nature. There have been included statements of the number and areas of parks, forests and game and fish refuges in each of the states, but here again, it must be remembered that it is difficult to get accurate figures, since, in some cases, the state authorities do not have the accurate figures. A further statement was presented, where the figures or estimates were available, of the extent to which the public was making use of these areas for recreation.

TABLE 4. SUMMARY DIGEST OF PROVISIONS OF STATE LAWS COVERING STATE PARKS, FORESTS AND RESERVATIONS

Key to Powers and Duties of Board: a, To Make Survey of Lands Available for Parks; b, To Administer State Park System; c, Condemnation; d, Purchase; e, To Contract with Cities, Counties, etc., for Care and Maintenance of Parks; f, To Accept Gifts, Donations, etc.; g, To Recommend to Governor Acceptance of Gifts of Forest Lands to State; h, To Transfer Lands to Local Authorities and to Receive Lands from Local Authorities; i, To Cooperate with Neighboring State Commissions; j, To Acquire Fish and Game Preserves.

State	Parks		Forests		Game and Fish Refuges		Power Vested in	Owned by Other than Governmental Agency	Powers and Duties of Board	Maintenance	Extent of Use by the Public for Recreation (Figures and Estimates)	Miscellaneous Provisions
	No.	Area (acres)	No.	Area (acres)	No.	Area (acres)						
Alabama	8	50	4	110			Forestry Dept., Dept. of Archives and History		g			
Arkansas	1	80					Park Board		a, b, c, f			
California	8	13,536					Dept. of Natural Resources (Park Board, Forestry Dept., Fish and Game Commission)		a, b, c, d, e, f		Calif. Redwood Park, average daily no. campers during entire season, 500; Humboldt Redwood Park during 1926 season, 30,000 people spent vacation	$6,000,000 bond issue voted to be submitted to voters in 1927 to acquire parks

State							Administration				
Connecticut	35	13	7,431		30,750		Park and Forestry Board		b, d, e, h, i, and c (not including forests)	appropriation	estimated attendance at 15 of 34 parks (Dec. 1, 1924–Nov. 30, 1926): visitors, 1,580,738; campers, 67,055
Delaware							Forestry Dept.				bill to provide Forestry Dept. and employ forester enacted 1927; appropriation $5,000
Florida	5		4,100				Forestry Dept.	private organizations aided by state			Forestry Dept. created by Act of 1927; provided two-year appropriation of $25,000 and employment of forester
Georgia		1		16			Forestry Dept.		f	occupation licenses and privilege taxes	
Idaho	1	1	7,838		177,545	3,000,000	Board of Public Works		b (Hepburn Park), appoint park supt.	concessions, camp site leases	visitors to park, 1926, about 30,000
Illinois	18	1		80			Conservation Dept. (incl. Forestry Dept. and Fish & Game Commission), Dept. of Forests and Waters, Dept. of Public Works		b, c, i, j (bond issue of $20,000,000 voted 1927)		summer 1926, more than 1,000,000 visitors to state parks and memorials

TABLE 4—*Continued*

State	Parks		Forests		Game and Fish Refuges		Power Vested in	Owned by Other than Governmental Agency	Powers and Duties of Board	Maintenance	Extent of Use by the Public for Recreation (Figures and Estimates)	Miscellaneous Provisions
	No.	Area (acres)	No.	Area (acres)	No.	Area (acres)						
Indiana	6	3,432	1	2,500	1	10,000	Conservation Department		b, c, f, h, j	tax levy, one mill for Forestry Fund; two mills annually for seven years for Indiana Dunes Park; admission to parks, 10c, concessions, camp site leases	attendance at three state parks, 1925: 138,452; 1926: 142,541	
Iowa	41	7,000	—		—		Conservation Department		b, c (parks), e, f, h (cities and counties aid in purchase of parks)	appropriation, $70,000 annually	five state parks had 600,000 visitors in 1926	
Kansas	5	1,350	—		—	16,000	Forestry Dept., Fish & Game Commission		f	receipts from fish and game licenses, concessions		
Kentucky	6	2,000	1	3,600	—		Park Board		a, b, f	10c admission to National Bridge Park. Louisville and Nashville R. R. pays to state monthly 10c for each adult and 5c for each child visiting this park		

					Conservation Department				
Louisiana	1	150	1	2,200	239,000; public hunting grounds, 23,000	Conservation Department				
Maine	8	270				State Land Agent and Forest Commissioner		f		estimated attendance at six forests 1926, 17,500
Maryland		6	6	6,000	34,310	Forestry Dept. under the State University				
Massachusetts	11	13,800	44	104,932		Conservation Dept., incl. Forestry Dept.	Trustees of Public Reservations, Appalachian Mountain Club, and nine other organizations	d, f	appropriation, admission fees (10c at Standish Monument), camp site leases	
Michigan	60	18,500				Conservation Dept., incl. Park Board, Forestry Dept., Fish and Game Comm. and Dept. of Forests and Waters		b, f, powers and duties of all depts. transferred to Conservation Dept.	appropriation, concession	visitors: 1924, 670,000; 1926, 2,539,672
Minnesota	22	38,872		350,000	90	Conservation Dept., incl. Forestry Commissioner, Comm. of Game and Fish, Comm. of Lands and Timber		b, c, d, f, i, to transfer federal lands, to withdraw from sale state lands, to perform all duties exercised by state auditor and forestry board	appropriation, tax levy, receipts from fish and game licenses, concessions	3,500,000 tourists visited state parks, spring and summer, 1926

TABLE 4—*Continued*

State	Parks No.	Parks Area (acres)	Forests No.	Forests Area (acres)	Game and Fish Refuges No.	Game and Fish Refuges Area (acres)	Power Vested in	Owned by Other than Governmental Agency	Powers and Duties of Board	Maintenance	Extent of Use by the Public for Recreation (Figures and Estimates)	Miscellaneous Provisions
Missouri	12	36,000					Fish and Game Commission		b, d	25% of receipts from fish and game licenses for parks	seven state parks had 19,929 registered visitors in 1927	
Montana			7	200,000			Forestry Dept. under Board of Land Commissioners		to exchange school lands for federal lands	appropriation, camp-site leases		
Nebraska	4	260					Park Board, under Dept. of Horticulture, Univ. of Nebraska		a, b, d, f	appropriation	two state parks had estimated attendance, summer 1927, 130,000	
Nevada					16	3,800,000	Fish and Game Commission		f, federal lands used by state	appropriation		
New Hampshire	1	8,000	52	21,283			Forestry Dept	Society for Protection of New Hampshire Forests, Appalachian Mt. Club	c, d, f	appropriation, camp-site leases	more than one million people use public reservations each season (est.)	

State					Administering agency	Cooperating agencies	Powers	Sources of revenue	Attendance	Remarks
New Jersey	5	11,438	6	18,954		Conservation Board, incl. Park Board and Forestry Dept.		a (approp. $5,000), b, d, f, powers do not extend over Palisades Inter-State Park or High Point Park	appropriation, camp-site leases	2,434 camping permits issued for a total of 3,193 camping weeks in Palisades Park, 1926	forest acquired by exchange of school lands for federal lands
New Mexico	—		1	10,000	70						
New York	89	Parks & Forests	—	2,147,102	1	Conservation Department	American Scenic and Historic Preservation Society, N. Y. Historical Society, and other semi-public and private agencies	b, c, d, f, h, i	appropriation, bond issues, concessions, camp-site leases, admission charges to parks	visitors to Harriman State Park and Bear Mt. Park, 1926, 4,660,581; camp capacity of Palisades Park, 1926, 1,920	
North Carolina	2	1,600		20,000	1	Department of Conservation and Development (incl. State Game Comm. and Fisheries Comm., Forestry Dept.			appropriation, concessions		game refuge is in federal forest, to be administered by state for ten years
North Dakota	13	170	—	—		Directors of State Historical Society					

TABLE 4—*Continued*

State	Parks		Forests		Game and Fish Refuges		Power Vested in	Owned by Other than Governmental Agency	Powers and Duties of Board	Maintenance	Extent of Use by the Public for Recreation (Figures and Estimates)	Miscellaneous Provisions
	No.	Area (acres)	No.	Area (acres)	No.	Area (acres)						
Ohio	5	30,000	15	35,000	88	100,000	Forestry Dept., Board of Public Works, Fish and Game Commission	State Archaeological and Historical Society	d, f	appropriation		
Oklahoma					1	16,000	Fish and Game Commission, Forestry Dept.		d, f			forestry program to be instituted
Oregon	17	636			3		State Highway Commission		c, d, f	state highway fund		
Pennsylvania	7	13,872		1,131,611	35	78,296	Dept. of Forests and Waters		b, c, d, e, h	appropriation, camp site leases, hunters licenses, (75c of each fee to be used to acquire game refuges),	31 public camping grounds, 1,300 permanent camp sites	
Rhode Island	19	1,215					Metropolitan Park Commission		b, c, d, f	appropriation, camp site leases		act creating forestry commission passed 1927, no appropriation

State						Forestry Dept.	de la Howe Industrial School	receive gifts, receive any funds from federal government		act creating forestry commission passed by 1926-27 legislature, no funds provided
South Carolina	1	1,000								
South Dakota	1	107,440		1	1	Park Dept., Forestry Dept., Fish & Game Comm.		d	appropriation, concessions, camp site leases	
Tennessee						Park and Forestry Board		a, b, c, d, f	appropriation	
Texas	52	30,821				Park Board		a, b, d, f	concessions	
Utah	1					Park Board		a, b, d, f		survey under way
Vermont	16	31,266	165	1	1	Conservation Dept., incl. Forestry Dept. and Fish and Game Comm., together with three persons appointed by Gov.		d, f	appropriation (1927: $24,500 for general forestry, $8,000 for purchase of forests), camp site leases	
Virginia	1	1,400	588	1		Park Board (incl. Forestry Dept., Geological commission)		d, f		
Washington	21	6,600	21,802			State Parks Committee, Forestry Dept.		b, c, d, e, f, may withdraw state lands from sale	appropriation, concessions, donations, 75 per cent of fines for violation of motor vehicle laws	

TABLE 4—*Concluded*

State	Parks		Forests		Game and Fish Refuges		Power Vested in	Owned by Other than Governmental Agency	Powers and Duties of Board	Maintenance	Extent of Use by the Public for Recreation (Figures and Estimates)	Miscellaneous Provisions
	No.	Area (acres)	No.	Area (acres)	No.	Area (acres)						
West Virginia	6	120	—		2	15,000	State Parks, Forests, and Conservation Commission		a, b			fish and game refuges purchased from revenues from hunting and fishing licenses
Wisconsin	12	85,740	—	331,000	—		Conservation Dept. incl. Forestry Dept. and Fish & Game Comm.		b, d, f	appropriation, concessions, camp site leases		
Wyoming	2	1,080	—		—		State Board of Charities and Reform			appropriation		

APPENDIX E

Note — The rankings were made on the following basis: with respect to delinquency, the district having the highest index was given rank number 1, the district with next highest, rank 2, and so on; in the matter of adaequacy, the district having the lowest adequacy index was given rank 1, that having the next highest, 2, and so on. The rankings were made in this order inasmuch as the object in comparison was to relate the districts having high delinquency indices with those having low percentages of play space, and those having high indices of play space adequacy with those having low delinquency ratios.

District	Delinquency Index Rank	Adequacy Index Rank	D^2 (Difference in rank squared)
1	1	21	400
2	11	10	1
3	14	13	1
4	17	7	100
5	4	5	1
6	6	9	9
7	7	1	36
8	12	23	121
9	8	4	16
10	16	11	25
11	3	3	
12	5	15	100
13	19½	27	56.25
14	28	19	81
15	19½	12	56.25
16	23	8	225
17	15	20	25
18	22	28	36
19	24	25	1
20	18	14	16
21	9	17	64
22	10	16	36
23	2	6	16
24	13	22	81
25	26½	18	72.25
26	21	26	25
27	25	2	529
28	26½	24	6.25
			2136

$$\rho(\text{rho}) = 1 - \frac{6 \times 2136}{28(28^2 - 1)} = 1 - .5845 = .42$$

$$r = + .44$$

[1] For method employed here, see Chaddock, R. E., *Principles and Methods of Statistics*, Houghton Mifflin Co., 1925, 471 pp., pp. 299-303.

TABLE B. CORRELATION BETWEEN DELINQUENCY AND CHILD DENSITY COMPUTED BY RANK METHOD

Play District	Child Density per acre	Rank	Delinquency Index Rank	D²
1	3.89	27	1	676
2	41.59	6	11	25
3	81.80	1	14	169
4	79.03	2	17	225
5	29.65	8	4	16
6	24.62	10	6	16
7	13.03	21	7	196
8	10.06	23	12	121
9	20.36	13	8	25
10	19.60	15	16	1
11	15.55	18	3	225
12	27.34	9	5	16
14	4.01	26	20	36
14	14.91	20	28	64
15	33.74	7	19	144
16	52.77	5	23	324
17	10.93	22	15	49
18	20.35	14	22	64
19	15.53	19	24	25
20	72.03	3	18	225
21	63.28	4	9	25
22	19.01	17	10	49
23	23.60	11	2	81
24	21.18	12	13	1
25	19.08	16	26	100
26	8.38	24	21	9
27	7.80	25	25	
28	2.43	28	27	1
				2908

$$\rho \, (\text{rho}) = 1 - \frac{6 \times 2908}{28 \, (28^2 - 1)} = 1 - .796 = .20$$

$$r = +.21$$

INDEX